THE St Michael PHOTOGRAPHY COURSE

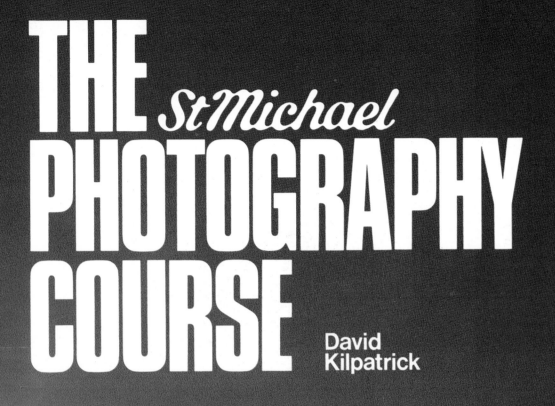

THE *St Michael* PHOTOGRAPHY COURSE

David
Kilpatrick

Contents

Title page: Shirley Kilpatrick

This edition published in 1984 for
Marks and Spencer p.l.c., Baker Street, London
by Newnes Books,
a Division of The Hamlyn Publishing Group Limited,
84-88 The Centre, Feltham, Middlesex

Copyright © Eaglemoss Publications Limited 1983
First published in *You and Your Camera*
Copyright © additional material for this edition; Newnes Books,
a Division of The Hamlyn Publishing Group Limited 1984

ISBN 0 600 35838 0

Printed in Italy

Equipment

To take better photographs, you need the right equipment. To select the right equipment, you need to know how it is used. The two go hand in hand. Starting out in photography, you can experiment with different cameras and lenses, films, techniques, subjects and ideas.

This book will help you select the best basic outfit to begin with, and follow through your progress as you learn to use it.

One thing, though, is always true in photography; the most important part is your own natural interest in the subject and the results. An interesting subject shot on simple equipment without special technical merit is more worthwhile than the most perfect image which fails to communicate. Most amateur photographs are dull because the subject is only of interest to the photographer and a limited circle of family or friends; they like it because it's part of their own experience.

A good photographer can picture exactly the same personal moments but make them visually strong, unexpected or even exciting. Learn to see, and to recognise picture potential; learn to choose and use the right equipment, materials and techniques. Become a better photographer, and your pictures will be appreciated by everyone.

Types of camera

There is a vast array of cameras on the market, so what are the main things to remember when choosing a new camera? Cameras range in complexity from easy-to-use elementary models to high precision instruments capable of recording a split second in the flight of a bumble-bee. The sort of camera you buy depends on what you want it to do for you—provide a record of your family or document the habits of an insect. So it is a case of choosing the type that is best for your kind of photography—and within your budget.

Choose wisely

Before you decide on a particular camera, try to do as much preliminary research as possible; ask your friends about their cameras and if possible gain first–hand experience by borrowing a camera from a friend, or the camera dealer may let you run a roll of film through the camera in the shop. Treat lavish advertisements with caution—do not buy a camera just because some famous photographer uses one—your type of photography may call for an altogether different piece of equipment. Make sure that, in practice, you need the specialized technical capabilities of a certain camera.

Ultimately, the quality of your photographs depends on a combination of factors, not just the performance of the camera. It depends on your ability to use the camera correctly, your personal judgement in 'seeing' a good picture and the quality of the film processing.

Counting the cost

When it comes to buying a camera, most photographers are price con-scious—what you might like to buy if you were left a legacy and what you can actually afford are often somewhat different. For a particular type of camera you will often find that there is a broad range of prices, so what might you expect to get for more money?

With any camera, but especially a 110 camera or a rangefinder camera, more money will get you a better lens. There will also be more controls. On simple cameras this may only amount to more shutter speeds but on SLR cameras the body may be designed to accept motor-drive, the lens mounting designed to accept different manufacturers' lenses and the exposure meter may provide both spot and general readings. And you would pay more for a more robust camera. If the camera you like is over your budget, don't dismiss the idea of buying a secondhand one. There are

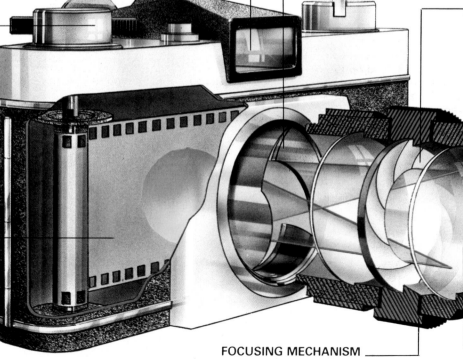

VIEWFINDER
A photographer views the subject through the viewfinder, which is a sighting device. It may have its own small lens or use a device which enables you to see through the camera's lens.

FILM ADVANCE
This device moves the film on by the correct distance after each exposure. In most cases, it is coupled to the shutter so if you forget to wind-on the shutter cannot be released. A frame counter records how many exposures you make.

FILM
The film, held flat inside the back of the camera, records the image. Both black and white and colour films are coated with light–sensitive emulsions which react in proportion to the amount of light that falls on them.

FOCUSING MECHANISM
This control moves the lens in and out to alter the distance between the lens and the film so that a sharp image of the subject falls on the film.

many bargains to be found in this market. A reputable dealer will probably ask more for a camera than a private seller but he should offer a written guarantee which makes it an attractive buy for those who are worried about the true condition of the camera.

The vital questions

To help you choose the right camera here are some of the points to consider. First, what subjects will you be photographing most of the time—moving subjects, such as sports events or children on the move, or portraits, still life and landscapes? Do you want a light, uncomplicated camera or are you prepared to carry a heavier camera with a full range of lenses?

Next, pick the camera up and handle it. Does it feel comfortable and can you hold it steadily? Make sure that you can reach all the controls, and that they are easy to operate. Don't accept that if a part is stiff or jerky it will 'work in'—try another camera.

Can you see the image comfortably in the viewfinder? Do you find it easier to compose well when you can see the exact edges of the picture or are you satisfied with the corner right angles in most 110, 126 and some rangefinder cameras? Think too about the film formats of different cameras: do you prefer square or rectangular pictures? Make sure the camera takes a good range of film types for the work you want to do.

If you intend to do your own processing, there is a wide range of equipment available for 35mm film, much less for 110/disc. If you want to make enlargements, the larger the negative size, the better the quality of the print. If you plan to project your colour transparencies, there is a wider range of projectors available for 35mm film.

Do you really need a heavy f1·4 lens which is mainly useful in poor light conditions? Most pictures are taken around f4 to f11 and a good quality f2·8 lens is better value than an indifferent f1·4 lens at the same price. Glamorous advertisements promote shutter speeds of 1/2000 which are only really necessary for scientific work; 1/500 is suitable for most general photography.

If you want to do close–up work or use telephoto lenses, you need a camera with interchangeable lenses. Are you intending to use flash? Then you need to discover the pros and cons of built-in flash versus a separate gun.

SHUTTER
This keeps light from the film until the instant of exposure. It also controls the length of time light falls on the film. Typically, it remains open for a fraction of a second. So a fast shutter speed and large aperture can allow the same total amount of light through as a slow shutter speed and small aperture.

APERTURE
The aperture is the circular hole in the middle of the lens through which light enters the camera. Its size can be altered to vary the amount of light entering the camera and falling on the film. Wide open it lets through as much light as possible, as would be necessary, for example, on a dull day. 'Stopped down' in very bright conditions it reduces the amount of light.

How cameras work

Every camera, from the simplest pocket-size model to the most sophisticated SLR, is basically a light-tight box with a piece of film at one end and a hole to let the light in at the other. The light is focused on to the film by a lens, forming an image of what is in front of the camera. The amount of light entering the camera is controlled by the size of the hole and the length of time it remains open. On top of the camera there is a viewing device that allows you to select the area of the subject to be included in the picture. Additions to this basic camera may make it more versatile but they are not essential.

LENS
The lens receives light reflected from the subject and focuses an inverted image on to the film. All but the simplest camera lenses have several separate elements working as one.

Check that it works

Whether you end up buying a new or secondhand camera it is advisable to test it before the guarantee runs out.

● Check all the shutter speeds; they should sound satisfactory and, if you open the back of the camera, you should be able to see the differences between the slower ones when the shutter is released. A specialist camera repairer will be able to test the shutter accurately.
● You can use the guide that comes with the film to cross-check that the exposure meter gives you the same information under the same conditions. But the best test is practical:

run a roll of film through the camera.
● Check the sharpness of the lens by running a roll of film through the camera. Include pictures focused at the closest distance, 5m and infinity.
● Make sure that the wind-on and film counter work accurately.
● Test the camera body for light-tightness by orientating it in various positions towards the sun.
● To test the camera's flash synchronization, take the back off the camera and look through the lens to see if the light from the flash coincides with the release of the shutter.
● The next four points are specifically for secondhand buyers:
● On an SLR camera always check the

condition of the focal plane blinds. To look for pinholes, remove the back of the camera and the lens, gently lift the mirror out of the way and hold the camera against a strong light while you slowly wind the shutter.
● The condition of the lens is also important so look at it obliquely to see if it has any scratches and check that there are no finger marks on it.
● Examine the general condition of the inside of the camera body and check that none of the screws is burred which may indicate that an amateur mechanic has been at work.
● If the camera has battery-powered controls, check that the batteries have not leaked and caused any corrosion.

1 EYE–LEVEL VIEWFINDER CAMERA
These are the simplest cameras, one step removed from the old box camera. You view the subject through a separate, small lens system, so you never see *exactly* the same view as the main camera lens. Framing marks in the viewfinder help to compensate for any parallax errors arising from this slight discrepancy.
For: many of these lightweight cameras are pocket–size. All are easy to use as the controls are minimal and usually keyed to simple symbols.
Against: these simple cameras are not suitable for close–up work or moving subjects and need flash in poor light. Lenses are not interchangeable but some models have supplementary lenses. On those models which focus, the distance between camera and subject must be guessed. If the camera has a fixed focus everything from about 2m to infinity is always in focus so you will not be able to have the subject sharp and the background blurred.

Film sizes: 110, 126, 135, 120, disc

2 RANGEFINDER CAMERA
This is a viewfinder camera with more advanced controls which sometimes include a built–in exposure meter. The rangefinder measures the distance the subject is from the camera for accurate focusing. The system of small lenses works in combination with those of the viewfinder so you see either a split or a double image in the viewfinder and turn the focus control until they line up accurately. These cameras give greater flexibility and quality than the simpler viewfinder models.
For: they are fairly easy to use and usually offer a wide range of shutter speeds suitable for most light conditions. Most take 35mm film which provides a wide choice of film type.
Against: only a few models have interchangeable lenses; the rest have fixed lenses, so are not suitable for close–up work. The image in the viewfinder, though bright, is small and sometimes difficult to focus.

Film sizes: 110, 135, 120, 220

3 SINGLE LENS REFLEX, 35mm PENTAPRISM CAMERA
This is the camera most widely used by both professional and serious amateur photographers. The SLR camera offers the most efficient viewing system. A mirror at 45° behind the lens directs the light upwards to a focusing screen. (The pentaprism turns the image right way round and up.) In this way you see the subject through the camera's lens, which eliminates parallax errors.
For: these cameras take a wide range of accessories which gives them great versatility. Focal plane shutters in front of the film allow the lens to be changed safely with a film in the

camera. A 35mm SLR is quick and easy to focus. The exposure metering is through the camera lens which is more accurate than a meter placed elsewhere on the camera body.
Against: the image is lost temporarily during exposure. A 35mm SLR cannot be used with electronic flash at fast shutter speeds which rules out 'fill–in flash' or 'synchro-sunlight' work with some films. They are heavier, bulkier and more complex than rangefinder cameras, and usually more expensive.

Film sizes: 135 (there are a few similar cameras that take other sizes of film)

4 ROLL FILM SLR CAMERA
The roll film SLR is favoured by many professionals. They have waist-level viewfinders but most also accept pentaprism and other viewfinders. Most produce 6 x 6cm negatives, which means the camera does not have to be turned on its side for vertical pictures. The models that produce oblong negatives are difficult to use vertically unless fitted with a pentaprism.
For: the bigger negative gives better quality than a 35mm negative. It is easy to see detail on a large viewing screen. Most models have interchangeable magazines or film-inserts that allow the camera to be reloaded very quickly. Some are fitted with between-lens shutters which are flash-synchronized at all speeds.
Against: extra lenses are heavy, bulky and expensive. When a waist-level viewfinder is used the image is reversed left to right. The basic camera is bulkier than a 35mm SLR.

Film sizes: 120 (6 x 6cm, 6 x 7cm, 4.5 x 6cm), 70mm double perforated

Pocket cameras, disc and 110

With such a choice of lenses and other accessories the 35mm SLR is hard to beat for its versatility. But what if you only need a camera to record some of the more memorable moments of an outing? You will not want to take an entire camera outfit, and even a compact SLR may be too bulky. In these situations a pocket camera comes into its own.

110 cameras

Most 110 cameras are small enough to fit in a jacket pocket or handbag. They all accept 110 cartridge films, which are available for colour prints and slides as well as black and white prints. Fast 400 ASA film is available for low light; medium speeds, like 64 and 80 ASA are for sunnier conditions. The cartridges are easy to load—they just drop into the camera back.

Because the frame size is so small, 0.5 × 0.7 (13 × 17mm), the films are fairly cheap to buy and equally light on the pocket when you have the films developed and printed.

Disc cameras are flat and square rather than long and slim, and more pocketable. Their 10 × 8mm frame size means even enprints show grain and lack fine detail. All disc cameras have built in motor wind and flash.

Disadvantages

Those who are looking for superior picture quality will be disappointed by such cameras. The biggest problem is the small film format. You can rarely have a big print made without the film's grain being noticeable.

Some cheap cameras have inferior quality lenses and slow fixed shutter speeds which cause fuzzy, blurred pictures. When you enlarge these neg-atives the fuzz and blur are increased too.

The lens in pocket cameras provides a fairly wide angle of view. Coupled with a fairly long minimum focusing distance, this can result in disappointing pictures. The subject comes out small in the frame, and is swamped by too much background.

Bearing in mind that most people choose a simple camera for snap-shot photography, you may be prepared to accept one or two shortcomings. If you take extra care over technique, or choose a camera with features to help, the pictures can be acceptable.

Cheapest cameras

Some 110 models are so inexpensive that they are almost disposable. You can even buy a kit to make your own.

▲ Upper left – a typical 110 camera with built in flash, the Minolta 450EX, with (lower left) the smallest pocket camera made, the Minox EC, which takes its own special film. Centre: sophisticated 110 with the Pentax Auto 110 Super, fitted flash, and two interchangeable lenses for SLR viewing. Right – high level disc (upper) with the Minolta Disc 7 featuring a viewing mirror to allow self portraits, and accepting a remote electronic release; basic disc (lower) with the Kodak 2000.

▼ Most simple cameras are fitted with a slightly wide angle lens and a small aperture, which is normally fixed. This gives the cameras a sufficiently large depth of field to allow for errors in focusing.

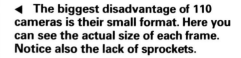

◀ The biggest disadvantage of 110 cameras is their small format. Here you can see the actual size of each frame. Notice also the lack of sprockets.

▲ A useful feature offered by some cameras is the macro facility. With the camera on normal setting, this is the closest you can get to this floral clock.

▲ By switching the focusing over to macro, you can move in on your subject and be as close as 10in (25cm). The carrying chain can be used to measure this distance.

▲ The Rollei A110 has an electronic flashgun that can be added on to the body and a built-in sensor to measure the required exposure. *Jack Schofield*

▲ The Minolta Weathermatic is designed for use under water as well as on dry land. It is also impervious to sand and is robust enough to survive heavy knocks. *Fran Saunders*

They make ideal gifts for young children and for people who don't want to fiddle with any type of control.

As you might expect, the cheapest cameras only have the most basic features. The lens is usually around 24mm in focal length, which is standard for 110 cameras. (It gives the same view as a 50mm lens on a 35mm camera.) Film is wound on by a rotating wheel. The focus is fixed; the closest you can approach the subject is about three feet (one metre). You can't generally adjust the exposure because both aperture and shutter speed are fixed. Apertures are normally between f8 and f11, whereas the shutter speed can be anywhere from 1/40 to 1/100, depending on the model.

Disc cameras have very basic exposure control; most have only two settings, one for daylight and one for low light which automatically fires the flash. the tolerance of the disc film covers all normal variations in light and the auto flash sharpens up dusk shots.

More money, extra features

By spending a little more you can buy a more versatile 110 camera which can cope better with variations in the level of light during a typical day. They usually have variable exposures using different shutter speeds, such as 1/50 for dull light and 1/100 for brighter conditions. The speed is often selected by a weather symbol (cloud symbols for dull weather, and so on).

In most cases the aperture is fixed.

These more expensive cameras may also have a quicker push/pull film wind lever, rather than a rotating wheel. Several have a plastic case which doubles as a handle for steadying the camera.

More valuable features available on one or two models are a built-in electronic flash gun which is far more

Special models

Some 110 format cameras have special features which make them stand out from the others. Three are shown here.

Minolta 110 Zoom SLR. This tiny camera has a 25-67 zoom lens (equivalent to a 50-135mm zoom on a 35mm camera). It has reflex viewing and focusing—you see what the lens sees. This allows precise framing and pin-sharp focus. Exposures are automatic using the aperture priority system. Many accessories, including flash, are available.

Pentax Auto 110. Like the Minolta model this camera has reflex viewing and focusing. What makes it so special is its interchangeable lens facility. Wide angle, standard and telephoto lenses are available and attach to the camera by a bayonet fitting. You can buy a complete outfit including auto-winder and flash gun. Exposures are fully automatic.

Minolta Weathermatic. Designed to be a 'fun camera', this conspicuous yellow model can safely take pictures underwater as well as on land. It also has a built-in flash gun which works on land or underwater. The body seals also keep out dust and sand.

convenient to use (and cheaper in the long run) than flash cubes or bulbs, and a 'telephoto' lens. The 'tele' facility is additional to the normal lens. It consists of an extra lens which slides into position over the normal lens to increase image magnification. Where the normal lens is 24mm for example, with 'telephoto' it becomes around 48mm, or twice the focal length. This can give more successful pictures of small subjects in the distance.

Versatility and price

If you are prepared to spend more, there is a long list of models with many different facilities. Some may have only one special feature, which costs you a little more, while the most expensive ones have just about everything you could hope for. The major 'extras' are as follows:

Dual lenses: some more expensive cameras have the telephoto facility of cheaper versions. One or two have a close-up facility. Most use a close-up lens which slides over the main lens and allows you to focus on closer subjects than normal — 10 inches (25cm) for example. This produces better pictures of small subjects.

Focusing: some models have variable focusing settings. These might be controlled by selecting the most appropriate focus symbol, by setting a specific distance on a scale, or by a rangefinder system where focus is correct when two viewfinder images superimpose.

Automatic exposure: this allows the camera to cope with a wider range of light levels than fixed exposure cameras. Most are controlled electronically and have a variable scale of shutter speed and aperture combinations. The shutter speed range might be 1/30 to 1/1000 and the aperture range f5·6 to f16 for example. In dull light the camera might choose 1/30 at f5·6; in bright light perhaps 1/1000 at f16. This is done automatically.

Built-in flash: electronic flash guns can now be made small enough to fit into the 110 camera body. Correct exposures are usually automatic, and the increase in price over a similar model without flash is minimal. They are convenient and popular and found in more and more new models.

Viewfinder information: with all these features present it is important that the photographer knows what is happening. Many models have a range of viewfinder signals: for example focusing symbol, battery check, low light (or slow shutter speed) warning, flash ready-to-flash, and 'parallax correction' marks to guide you when framing a close subject.

Other features: nowadays you can buy a 110 model with perhaps more features than some 35mm SLRs. Motorized film advance, tripod socket, delayed action timer, battery check, cable release, aperture- or shutter-priority automatic exposures and date imprint facilities are no longer rarities.

Using small formats

Recognise your camera's capabilities *and* limitations and work within them. *Do not* try to take pictures in dim light with fixed exposure cameras; don't have big enlargements made from the negatives; don't go closer than the minimum focusing distance.

Do get as close as you can to use all of the picture area effectively; do observe all the rules and tips for good composition (like varying camera angle, aiming for balanced in pictures, and so on); do use fast film when light is low; do use flash for indoor pictures; do steady the camera against something solid whenever possible.

Buy a camera which has all the features you want and no more. Ask yourself if you really want flash, motorized film advance and a telephoto lens facility, or would a smaller selection of extras be more suited to your budget.

35mm compact cameras

The popularity of 35mm compact cameras is growing all the time. This is not surprising, as they can fulfill a great variety of needs. These cameras are small, light, and most will fit into a small space, such as a pocket. Some offer a high degree of automation, including automatic exposure control, built-in automatic flash, auto-focusing, motorized film advance and even motorized rewinding of the film. This makes them very simple to use. And yet, the 35mm compact can produce results that are as good as those from an SLR camera. It can, therefore, be used as a photographic tool in its own right, or as a back-up to a comprehensive SLR system.

Types of compact

Manual cameras: by far the smallest group of 35mm non-reflex cameras is the manual exposure type. The cheapest ones have no light meter but often provide you with weather symbols (bright sun and cloud for example). Most, however, have some form of metering. The photographer then has to set shutter speed and aperture according to the film speed and lighting to get a correct exposure. Correct settings are confirmed by a meter scale, pointer or LED (light emitting diode).

Auto-exposure cameras: this is the biggest group. Most of these cameras have a meter cell under a tiny window in the lens surround. This is generally coupled to the ASA selector dial so that when you set a slow speed like 25 ASA, a small hole in a perforated disc is placed over the light sensitive cell. The light meter is connected to the exposure controls for aperture and shutter speeds. It automatically sets the correct exposure for the surrounding light. Different systems are used in some models, but all have the same end—that of making correct exposures easy.

A few cameras have a manual override option. This allows you to switch from automatic and set the exposure you want to use to suit the subject—perhaps for shallow depth of field or creative movement blur.

Built-in flash

Many models have a hot shoe or cable socket for flash, but built-in electronic flash is increasing in popularity. Including a flash in the camera body puts up the price surprisingly little. The flash is tiny, and so doesn't add much in the way of weight or bulk. Having flash on hand is convenient because it's one less item to carry.

The flash units are powered by one or two small penlight batteries. Exposures are generally set automatically. The system usually works on the focusing distance you've set, varying the lens aperture to give correct exposures.

▶ With compact cameras, the controls are usually placed around the lens barrel. Unlike 35mm SLRs, none is on the top plate. The model shown here is one of the most sophisticated 35mm compacts. The lens barrel has a focusing scale, automatic shutter-priority exposure and a full range of shutter speeds and film speed settings.

1 Minolta CLE has three interchangeable lenses
2 Konica AA half-frame compact takes up to 72 18 × 24 shots per roll
3 Ricoh FF-3 is fully automated
4 Balda 35C has detachable flash unit
5 Minolta AF-Sv has synthesized 'voice' warnings

Compact cameras are ideal for carrying around on the off-chance of catching a candid shot or recording something of interest.

▶ **Kids fishing, taken with a Rollei 35T on Agfa CT18.**

▼ **Country cottage, using a Minolta Hi-matic 7SII Auto. Pictures by** *Raymond Lea*

When built-in flash is provided the PC sync socket is usually omitted. This limits you to using direct flash in dim lighting. As the flash is fairly close to the lens you may get 'red-eye'. The small size of the units limits their power output—you must work within strict distance limits to avoid under-exposure and flash fall-off at the edges of the picture. Also, you cannot angle the tube to bounce and soften the lighting.

General features

Compacts range from very cheap models to some which cost more than many 35mm SLRs. Manual and automatic exposure cameras are found throughout the price range. What price does decide, however, is overall quality of lens and body, plus the number of extra features.

Film advance: the cheaper cameras have a thumb wheel which you turn to advance to the next frame. Spend slightly more and you'll get the convenience of a film lever which is much quicker to use. A few have a built-in power winder.

Shutter speed range: some cameras have only one shutter speed (*eg* 1/125), some give you a choice of perhaps three and 'B' for long exposures, while others have a wide range from 1/30 to 1/500 and more. Such ranges are generally found on cameras with between-lens leaf shutters. A few non-reflex cameras have focal plane shutters with ranges from 1 second to 1/1000.

Aperture range: the wider the maximum aperture of the lens the more expensive the camera tends to be. It is usually around f3·5 though some go as wide a f1·7. Smallest apertures are about f16, occasionally f22.

Lens: the focal length supplied, at around 40mm, is slightly wide angle for the 35mm format. Very few non-reflex cameras have interchangeable lenses. Some have retractable lenses—which push in flush with the camera body—so that they can be folded away for extra protection when not in use. This also makes them smaller and easier to pocket.

Focusing: most of the current models have adjustable focusing. The usual minimum distance is around 3 feet (1 metre). You either set a distance scale or select a particular focusing symbol, while some cameras provide both. The more expensive models may have rangefinder focusing. You have to turn the focusing ring until two images in the viewfinder are superimposed.

Viewfinder: the picture area is generally outlined by a bright frame inside which all your compositions should fall. For close subjects the camera has to be moved up and slightly left to avoid framing errors. Parallax marks are normally given to show you how to re-frame. Depending on the specifications of the camera, you might also see exposure settings (aperture and/or shutter speed), or simply 'exposure correct' signals flanked by an under and over-exposure warning. Sometimes a lamp glows if the shutter speed falls below a safe setting for hand holding. A battery check and focusing symbols might also appear in the viewfinder.

Miscellaneous features: you can expect to find a tripod socket, a rotating crank for rewinding film and an additive frame counter which registers frames up to 36 exposures and slightly beyond. Some cameras also have a delayed action timer, a cable release socket, and a shutter lock to prevent wasted frames. With some electronic cameras the shutter doesn't work unless there is sufficient battery power.

Special features

As well as power-wind, built-in flash and fully automatic exposures, you can find one or two cameras with extra features. Some have a device which you can switch on to print a date or code in one corner of your pictures. Some have a small window in the camera back to show what film you are using, while others have a signal to confirm that film is going through the camera properly.

Some automatic cameras have an exposure lock to give a useful degree of control over exposures for difficult conditions. With this system for example, you can take a reading close to the

subject, then step back to reframe the picture, holding the correct exposure for the important area of the subject. You might also be provided with a backlight compensation button: pressing this automatically gives a backlit scene more exposure to prevent it from becoming a silhouette. Some models have automatic film loading and re-winding.

Limitations

Experienced users of SLR cameras may find some features on a non-reflex camera frustrating. The major drawback is the fixed lens. You are stuck with a slightly wide angle view which takes in rather more of a scene than a standard lens would. You can't change the lens for telephoto or ultra-wide angle effects. This is made worse by a fairly long minimum focusing distance. It is difficult to compensate for the small magnification of a wide angle by getting in close—you can't because the subject goes out of focus.

The lack of a reflex view—you don't see exactly what the lens sees—can cause one or two problems. You may not notice flare or something obstructing the lens, for example. It is possible to take pictures with the lens cap on! Also, when focusing close to the subject it is easy to cut off part of the subject by mistake. You must move the camera slightly to correct for this 'parallax error' caused by having a separate viewing lens.

Sometimes you may want to use a slow shutter speed or small aperture for specific effects. With programmed shutters (which many automatic-exposure

models have) low light shots are taken at wide apertures and slow speeds, whereas bright scenes are recorded at a small aperture and fast speed. You normally have no control over the actual settings.

Make the most of it

The main advantages of a compact 35mm are that it is portable, quick, and very quiet to use. Many SLR owners carry a compact camera when on holiday or short outings. This saves the bother of carrying a lot of heavy equipment they probably won't use, but lessens the risk of missing that 'once in a lifetime' picture.

The compact also has more positive uses. As it is quiet, it attracts less attention than an SLR, and can be used for candid photography more easily. As auto-exposure compacts are so quick to operate, they can be used to 'grab' shots that might be missed with a more complex SLR.

Also, you can fit filters and 'special effects' accessories to a compact to add a creative dimension to your photography. You can't see the effect in the viewfinder, but experience will guide you. Close-up lenses will allow you to take impressive close-ups, and so on. And you can use all the lessons you have learned about composition—they apply to all cameras, regardless of cost.

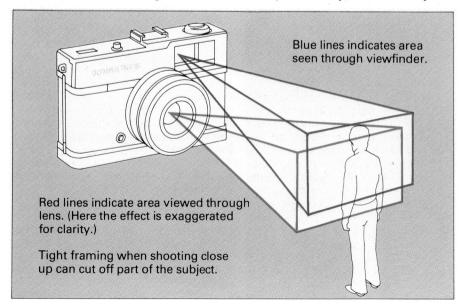

Blue lines indicates area seen through viewfinder.

Red lines indicate area viewed through lens. (Here the effect is exaggerated for clarity.)

Tight framing when shooting close up can cut off part of the subject.

◀ ▲PARALLAX ERROR
Since 35mm compacts are not reflex cameras, the image in the viewfinder is not quite the same as that on the film (left). This is called parallax error. To overcome it, some models have parallax marks on the viewfinder screen. When photographing a subject close to you, make sure it is framed within these marks, as above.

35mm SLR cameras

With its accurate viewing and focusing system, through–the–lens (TTL) metering, and interchangeable lens facility providing scope for almost every picture–taking situation, it is easy to see why the 35mm SLR is a popular general purpose camera. There is a vast number to choose from, and the competition in terms of specification, quality and price is keen.

There are a number of points to consider before spending your money.

● What is the most you can afford to spend?

● What type of exposure metering do you want?

● Is the viewfinder easy to use?

● Are the controls convenient?

● Are the shutter speed and aperture ranges adequate for your purposes?

● Does the camera allow you to build up a worthwhile system (particularly lenses)?

Price

Decide on your price limit, and stick to it. Only you can know how much you can afford to spend, not the person from whom you are buying. It is worthwhile spending an hour or so scanning through dealers' advertisements to see how much prices vary for the camera you would like to buy. Remember that the price of a camera often reflects the price of accessories you will want to add later. Try to think ahead; can you afford a system?

Exposure measurement

Almost all SLRs today have TTL metering, and light readings are taken from light passed by any focal length lens. (External or hand–held meters can be time–consuming to use.)

A full aperture metering camera can take light readings with the lens set at its widest aperture. The viewfinder therefore remains bright for ease of focusing and composition, and is closed down to the correct aperture only when the shutter is released.

Stopped–down metering means that an accurate reading can only be taken at the working aperture and, although cheaper, this system is not as convenient to use as is full–aperture metering.

Manual or automatic?

Do you want the built–in meter to give automatic or manual exposure settings? With a manual camera the photographer has to decide on the combination of aperture and shutter speed to provide a correct exposure. This gives the photographer total control, but time can be lost in setting both camera controls. Automatic exposure systems can be far quicker to use.

If you decide to buy one of the many cameras offering automatic exposure setting, consider whether you prefer aperture of shutter priority systems of operation. Multi-mode cameras

have a choice of both systems; some can also programme both settings without the photographer having to do anything except set the film speed, compose and focus. Automatic use means that if lighting conditions are constantly changing the exposure is instantly and automatically adjusted.

Viewfinder

The SLR is built around its viewing system, so the viewfinder is an important feature. A large rearsight enables spectacle wearers to see the whole screen clearly—if a rubber eye cup can be fitted this is often more comfortable to use.

Focusing screens vary in construction, some being brighter and more evenly illuminated than others. Dim, uneven focusing screens can hamper accurate focusing.

A few cameras have interchangeable screens and viewfinders, but most people can manage quite happily with the ground–glass screen, microprism circle and split image centre spot commonly seen in many modern SLR cameras.

Also often shown in the viewfinder are the shutter speed, lens aperture, or both. Over– and under–exposure warnings and correct exposure signals are almost always featured. Such complete viewfinder information shows the exposure situation at a glance.

Some manual cameras only have a

▲ The 42mm screw thread lens mount is now usually only found on cheaper manual cameras. To ensure correct focus the lens must be completely screwed in. Changing screw-in lenses can be time-consuming.

▲ Many cameras in all price ranges have bayonet lenses. First align the two reference dots: three claws on the lens then mate with three slots in the camera mount. A short twist locks in the lens for full exposure coupling.

▲ ▶ Metering at full aperture ensures a bright viewing image whatever aperture is set, but depth of field is difficult to judge without a preview.

▲ ▶ Stopped-down meter readings always darken the viewfinder image according to the aperture set; depth of field can be seen but focusing may be difficult.

◀ Whether you choose full-aperture or stopped-down metering, exposure results should be identical. Decide if you want economy or convenience.

correct exposure indication, with no other exposure information provided. This system demands that you know the camera well enough to judge which shutter speed and aperture you have set without removing your eye from the eyepiece.

Pointer needle meter displays can often be interpreted more accurately than light emitting diodes (LEDs), so that with experience you can deliberately make small exposure adjustments, perhaps only ⅓ stop, without looking at the aperture or shutter speed dials. Black needles can, however, be much more difficult to see than LEDs in dim light, or against a dark subject area.

Handling

Once you have decided on the type of camera you would like to buy by checking price and specification, you will probably have a short–list of two or three different cameras. From then on your choice becomes far more sub-jective, and you can only make your final decision based on how you feel about the handling of each camera.

Size, bulk, weight and layout of con-trols are all matters of personal pre-ference. Some people prefer a shutter

A small, light camera is not necessarily superior to a large, heavier one; base your choice on how you feel about holding and handling both types.

speed dial to be on the camera top plate, for example, whereas others like a shutter speed ring to be around the lens mount. Both types are available.

A bright viewfinder and ease of fine focusing are equally important—but you can only judge if these aspects are up to your standards by going to a dealer and handling a number of cameras.

Spend a little time with each of your short–listed cameras in your hands to feel how the film advance lever, aperture and shutter speed controls, automatic and manual metering, and depth of field preview operate.

Shutter

If you take action pictures the camera's fastest shutter speed is important. Top speeds of 1/1000 (more rarely 1/2000) can freeze fast motion. If much of your photography is in low light then the choice of speeds at the slow end of the range is more important.

Speeds may be controlled electronically or mechanically. Automatic electronic cameras often have a shutter speed range down to 8 or 16 full seconds, and shutter speeds can be infinitely variable (or 'stepless') through the range. If a mechanical speed is also provided (some cameras have more than one) you can make an exposure even if the batteries fail—but

the meter will no longer operate.

Most focal plane shutters synchronize for flash at 1/60 or slower, but some allow use of 1/125 to give more exposure choice when you use fill–in flash.

Noise and vibration are important considerations, especially to the wildlife or candid photographer, and lack of vibration is especially important when using slow speeds or telephoto lenses.

Powered film advance imposes extra strain on mechanical shutters and mirror movements, and cameras have to be constructed more robustly to cope with this. While most bodies are robust enough to cope with the modest 2fps rate of an autowind, stronger construction is needed for the more rapid shooting rates required by motor–drives. Go on brand reputation and whether the main body and controls have a substantial feel to them.

Lenses

The majority of 35mm SLR cameras have bayonet fitting lenses. Few now retain the once universal 42mm screw thread because, although the lenses tend to be slightly cheaper, it takes longer to unscrew one lens and screw in another than the more rapid twist–lock bayonet action.

Bayonet fittings for different camera brands vary, and specific types are

rarely (if ever) interchangeable between different makes of camera. The major exception is the Pentax-K bayonet design from Asahi which is now featured on several other camera names. There are also ranges of lenses by independent manufacturers made to fit cameras of varying bayonet designs. You almost always have to buy a camera with its standard lens. This is often 50 or 55mm in focal length, but 40 and 45mm standard lenses with their slightly wide angle view are gaining in popularity.

Common maximum apertures, in order of cost, are f1·2, f1·4, f1·8 and f2. A wide maximum aperture gives a slight exposure edge in dim light, but you may prefer to use a fast film than to buy a more expensive lens which, in practical terms, can only give perhaps an extra half stop.

Lenses often sell on reputation—but for good reasons. It is therefore better to go for well–known makes when choosing lenses rather than the cheapest one you can find. Take bulk and weight into account when buying additional lenses—both should complement the camera body.

If you aren't obliged to buy the standard lens with the camera body, consider buying a zoom which takes the 50mm focal length in to its focal length range. It will doubtless cost more than a

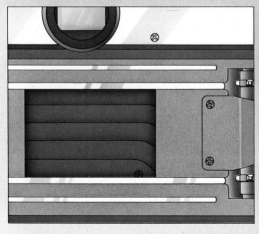

▶ Consider the layout of controls. Perhaps you prefer a shutter speed ring around the lens.

▶ A shutter speed dial on the top plate is more common. Large controls can be easier to use.

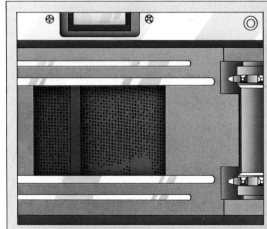

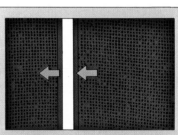

HORIZONTAL SHUTTER
Left: cocking the shutter pulls the blinds over the film. Above: the slit moves horizontally across the film during exposure. Flash sync is around 1/60.

VERTICAL SHUTTER
Left: construction is usually of metal blades. Above: the slit moves vertically during exposure. The short travel enables fast flash sync speeds.

standard lens, but by no means as much as several lenses encompassed by the zoom range.

Choosing

Consider first that the camera will be the heart of your outfit, so ensure a good range of reasonably priced lenses and accessories are readily available from the manufacturer and from independent makers. Even more important, make sure that the camera suits your requirements, that it is comfortable to hold, and that the controls are of a suitable size with clear lettering where applicable.

Operation should be easy, not a task. Don't be too influenced by flashing coloured lights, bleeping signals, and a 'professional' finish. These can be useful, but none of them make better pictures. Remember that the more LEDs there are, the greater the drain on the batteries—batteries can be expensive.

Bargains can often be had by buying a second–hand camera. Many dealers offer discount on new equipment and this can provide a useful saving. In any event, don't expect to combine the maximum discount with the maximum of after–sales service. It is rarely possible, and your dealer's advice as you progress is usually worth your paying that little extra.

Automatic 35mm SLRs

Top row: left, basic aperture priority and manual from the Ricoh XR-7; centre, the Minolta X-500 adds off the film flash metering to this specification; right, the 139MD Quartz goes further and has a built-in film winder too. Bottom row: Olympus's OM-10 is auto- only but converts to manual by adding an adaptor. Centre, the Pentax Super A has multiple exposure modes and a choice of fully automatic programmes. Right, the Canon T50 is fully programmed with auto film loading and wind-on in a new style body shell.

Incorrect exposure is the most common cause of spoiled pictures. Automatic exposure systems, however, offer the simplest, most convenient means of consistently getting the exposure right for most subjects and lighting conditions. More important, automation allows you to concentrate on the most important aspect of photography—the subject.

There are two basic types of automatic exposure control: shutter priority and aperture priority (sometimes called shutter– or aperture–preferred). In both cases the photographer sets one control and the camera computes the other. A few cameras have a fully automatic arrangement programmed to select both settings.

As with any separate or built–in light meter, the automatic exposure system must be pre–set with the ASA speed of the loaded film for accurate exposures. In other words, set the film speed dial correctly before you begin taking photographs.

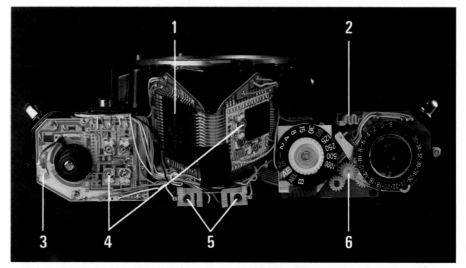

▲ An inside view of what makes automation possible—electronics. A complicated array of circuits and wires control the functions of the multi–mode Fujica AX–5. Don't be tempted to tamper—a costly repair may result.

1 Main control centre (micro chip)
2 Contacts for shutter release button
3 On/off and delayed action switches
4 Meter and shutter speed resistors
5 Hot shoe/dedicated flash contacts
6 Cogs for reverse frame counting

Shutter priority

The photographer chooses a shutter speed suitable for the subject and the effect required, and the automatic system selects and sets the correct aperture. The aperture settings are stepless (not limited to full or half stops) to give precise exposures even in rapidly changing light conditions.

Advantages: the user can choose a sufficiently fast shutter speed to arrest movement of a subject, or to avoid camera shake under poor lighting conditions. Intentional blur can also be produced to create the impression of movement by selecting a slow speed.

Disadvantages: you tend to get shallow depth of field in dim lighting; much greater depth of field results when the light is strong. If a particular aperture is required to control depth of field, the shutter speed dial must be adjusted until the viewfinder meter display shows the aperture you need. This delays picture taking.

Light metering, viewing and focusing can all be carried out with the lens at full aperture, but only lenses with the correct couplings can be used to ensure that the lens closes down to the automatically selected aperture for each exposure. Fixed aperture lenses such as mirror lenses therefore cannot be used on 'automatic'.

Applications: the system is ideal for the sports or wild–life photographer whose work depends to a great extent on using the correct shutter speed to freeze movement, and for photographers who want to introduce a controlled degree of blur.

Set for shutter priority automatic

▲ When stopping the action counts, a shutter priority camera comes into its own. You select a sufficiently fast shutter speed and the correct aperture is set automatically according to the lighting conditions.

▶ Shutter priority automatic use is only possible with the lens aperture ring set on 'AE'. Rotate the shutter speed dial to select the most suitable speed for the subject. Moving the ring off 'AE' switches to manual exposures.

Aperture priority

The photographer sets the aperture of his choice and the automatic exposure system sets the appropriate shutter speed for the lighting conditions and the film in use. The shutter speed scale in the viewfinder only gives an approximate indication of the speed selected because most automatic aperture cameras have stepless shutter speeds. This means that speeds are infinitely variable throughout the range instead of only those fixed settings marked on a dial.

Advantages: the system is ideal for immediate control over depth of field. Large apertures can be set to limit sharpness, making a subject stand out from an out of focus background. Small apertures can be set enabling most of the subject to be sharp in the photograph. If a lens has a fixed aperture (for example a mirror lens) an aperture

Set for aperture priority automatic

priority camera will still give automatic exposures by varying the shutter speed.
Disadvantages: you can get blur and camera shake in dim lighting, and frozen action pictures in bright conditions. When a particular speed is required, to avoid camera shake for example, you have to juggle with apertures until the appropriate shutter speed shows in the viewfinder. This takes time, and one advantage of automation—speed—is lost.

◄ With an aperture priority automatic camera select 'A' (for automatic) on the shutter speed dial. The correct shutter speed is automatically set to match the aperture you have selected. Move the dial off 'A' for a full range of manually selected exposures.

▼ Aperture priority cameras are ideal for controlling depth of field.

Applications: aperture priority cameras are by far the most common automatics, and they can be used for a wide variety of subjects. They are ideal for work involving accurate control of depth of field, for example close–ups using extension tubes when the lens is mounted some distance from the camera body, or even for microscope work when the camera lens isn't used at all.

Multi–mode cameras

Some cameras can be switched to either aperture priority or shutter priority, and may have additional exposure facilities. For example:
● automatic flash exposures
● automatic exposures with the lens stopped down
● fully programmed automatic exposures where the camera selects both aperture and shutter speed
● manual control of exposure

Advantages: obviously a multi–mode camera is extremely versatile. It has all the advantages of shutter and aperture priority cameras, but can be set to 'programmed' (P) to allow the photographer to concentrate totally on composition.

Disadvantages: multi–mode cameras are more expensive than their simpler counterparts, but their only real disadvantage is that, until you are familiar with all the controls and viewfinder

▶ **With up to six choices of exposure mode (including manual) a multi–mode camera may at first seem complicated, but familiarity breeds confidence. Here 'P' (programmed) has been set.**

▼ **On 'P' the camera sets both shutter speed and aperture, so you need only compose and focus. In allowing quick operation 'P' is ideal for candid shots.**

Set to programmed exposure

▲ Automatic–only aperture priority cameras are easily identified by the lack of a shutter speed dial. When you have set an aperture the camera automatically sets the correct shutter speed. 'B' for timed exposures and a flash setting are also provided. In this case 'M90' is for flash, and also provides a mechanical emergency shutter speed in case the batteries fail.

◄ The 'dedicated' or 'integrated' flash gun is designed for maximum convenience with automatic cameras. When both the camera and flash are set to automatic, and the flash is fully charged, the correct shutter speed to synchronize with flash is set automatically. This ensures that you do not inadvertently set too fast a shutter speed, and spoil your flash shot.

displays, photography can be confusing.

Applications: these cameras are designed to cope with almost any photographic situation. A multi–mode camera can be used for most types of photography as well as becoming a 'family camera', mode selection depending on the ability or interest of the user.

Manual override

Many automatic cameras can also be used completely manually. Whether there is a moving needle or LED (light emitting diode) display in the viewfinder, on the manual setting you adjust the camera controls until a 'correct' exposure is indicated, just as with a manual exposure camera, giving you full control over exposures.

For manual exposures with a shutter priority camera you move the lens aperture ring off its automatic setting. With aperture priority cameras, you turn the shutter speed dial from the automatic position to set a selected speed. Both types of camera usually have a locking device to prevent this from happening accidentally.

Automatic override

No automatic system can cope with all lighting and subject conditions, or allow for the photographer's personal preferences. Most automatic cameras have some means of modifying the settings made by the exposure system, while retaining the automatic facility (in other words without having to switch to manual operation).

An exposure compensation scale often surrounds the film speed dial, and adjusting this gives a little more or a little less exposure by effectively changing the film speed setting. Setting '+1' or 'x2' (depending on how the scale is marked) gives one stop more than—or double—the metered exposure, while '–2' or 'x¼' provides two stops less than—or one quarter of—the metered exposure.

Automatic–only cameras

A number of aperture priority automatic cameras do not offer manual control. Some automatic exposure override is normally featured, although in some cases this is limited to a fixed 1½ stops increase in exposure for backlit subjects.

Although there is no conventional shutter speed dial, a control on the top plate is usually marked in the following way: 'A' for automatic exposures, 'B' for long exposures, 'X' or '60' for a flash synchronization speed. There is often an 'off' position, and sometimes settings for one or more mechanical shutter speeds.

Flash guns

Some manufacturers market special 'dedicated' or 'integrated' flash units specifically for use with their range of automatic cameras. The flash is mounted on the camera hot shoe and the camera and flash are first set to 'auto'. When the flash is fully charged the camera is automatically set to the correct flash synchronization speed. All you have to do is to choose a suitable aperture.

Most automatic cameras accept a large number of electronic flash guns, but some of them lack an X socket. An extension sync cable cannot be used, and unless prepared to buy a hot shoe adaptor with extension cable, the photographer is therefore limited to hot shoe mounted flash photography.

Understanding the lens

► The lens illustrated is the type usually fitted to an SLR camera. It encompasses more or less the same view you see with one eye closed. The information on the front of the lens gives its focal length (50mm), maximum aperture (f2), maker's name, brand name, and serial number. The side view shows scales for focusing, aperture setting and depth of field.

Modern lenses are made up from several glass elements ground to a precise shape and mounted inside a tube.

▼ The 110 camera usually has a lens with a similar view to the 50mm lens above but the focal length is shorter because of the film's small size.

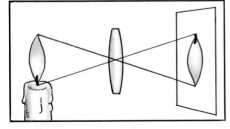

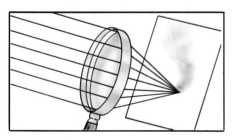

▲ With an object at infinity, such as the sun, light rays become parallel. The distance between a magnifying glass and the paper as it scorches— when the rays are focused—is the focal length of the lens.

▲ A candle flame is much closer than the sun so its light rays are not yet parallel on reaching the magnifying glass. To focus sharply on the flame the lens must be moved further from the paper.

The lens focuses light on to the film to form an image, and unless that image is sharp you will never produce clear pictures. So it is important to understand how the lens works, and what your particular lens can do. Only when you feel comfortable with the lens controls and can adjust them quickly and accurately will you get the most enjoyment and satisfaction out of trying out different effects in photography.

Focal length

The amount of a scene photographed by any lens is governed by its focal length. On a 35mm camera a normal lens of 40-50mm has roughly the same view as the human eye. To photograph more of the subject, or to pull distant objects closer, you need lenses with different focal lengths. The shorter focal length (under 35mm) of the wide angle lens gives a broad view of the scene, while the much longer focal length of a telephoto lens shows up detail in distant objects. Focal length is the distance between the lens and the film when the lens is focused at infinity (for a normal lens, that means set for objects more than 30m away). You can set fire to a piece of paper by holding a magnifying glass at exactly the point where a sharp image

of the sun (at infinity) forms on the paper, and a camera lens focuses an image on film in the same way. In each case, the distance between the lens and the image is the focal length.
Now imagine a magnifying glass forming the image of a candle flame on a sheet of paper. The distance between paper and glass before a sharp image is formed is greater than when the sun's rays are used. The closer an object is to the camera, the further the lens must be from the film to focus correctly.
Most simple 110 and 126 cameras have lenses with no focusing adjustment. These have been factory set to keep everything sharp between 2m and infinity. Most 35mm cameras have lenses which must be accurately focused by the photographer. These are set in helical mounts, two telescoping tubes with a screw thread between them. The closest focusing distance is determined by the maximum movement of this mount: for example, the shortest distance a 50mm lens fitted to a 35mm reflex camera focuses at is usually about 30–50cm.
If you have a reflex camera, try this yourself by setting the lens to minimum distance and moving backwards and forwards until an object close by be-

focusing ring

scale for focusing
(in metres and feet)

depth of field scale
(colour coded)

aperture settings
(f numbers)

lens mount
(where lens fits into camera body)

DEPTH OF FIELD SCALE
On this lens the depth of field scale is colour coded to correspond with the relevant f number. You can see that f16, for example, is shown in blue and so is the depth of field marking for that aperture setting. Other lenses may use diverging black lines running from each f number to the depth of field scale.

comes sharp in the viewing screen. Then measure the distance in between.

Normal lenses

The standard lens fitted to a camera is referred to as normal because, like the human eye, it takes in a 45–50° section of the scene. The focal length is usually more or less equal to the diagonal of the negative. Negative size varies, so the focal length of a normal lens depends on the film size a camera takes. In a 35mm camera the normal or standard lens is between 40–50mm, but for a small pocket camera taking 110 film it need only be 25mm.

The larger format cameras have correspondingly longer focal-length normal or standard lenses.

Brightness control

The brightness of the light reaching the film is controlled by a hole called the aperture. It works like the pupil of the eye, large in the dark to let in more light and small in bright conditions. The camera lens controls its aperture with a diaphragm (a mechanical iris) which is operated by a ring or lever outside the lens. The dimmer the light the larger the aperture must be to keep the brightness of the light on the film constant.

f numbers

Simple cameras often mark the aperture control with weather symbols, but the more complex cameras use a numerical system called f numbers. The smaller the f number, the larger the aperture; for example, f2·8 lets in more light than f5·6 and much more than f16. (The next chapter describes this more fully.)

Depth of field

Changing the f number also affects the depth of field, or amount of the scene in front of the camera that appears in focus. The depth of field scale on the lens indicates how much of the area in front of and behind the subject is in focus. If you move the aperture ring on the lens through the range of f numbers you can see how this control over sharpness can be used to subdue unwanted background and emphasize the main subject or, at a smaller aperture, to take a picture which is sharp from foreground to infinity.

Caring for your lens

● Never touch the lens surface. Greasy fingermarks are hard to remove.

● Use a soft lens brush to remove dust particles from the lens, or polish lightly with a rolled up, lint-free cloth, moving from rim to centre.

● Never clean your lens with solvent. If absolutely necessary, flood the glass surface with distilled water, invert the lens, and blot dry carefully.

● If you drop the lens in water, sand, or mud, dry it gently and take it to a camera shop for cleaning. Do not dismantle it yourself.

● Always replace the case or lens cap after use. When changing lenses, put the rear cap on and look after your lens mount fitting.

● Never oil the moving parts of your lens.

● A skylight or UV/haze filter kept permanently on the lens is a sensible protection against dust particles.

● Always keep your lenses in a cool, dry place.

Changing the angle of view

The angle of view, or the amount of a scene taken in by the lens, is governed by the focal length of the lens; for example, a short focal length will give a wide angle or view. So you can photograph different parts of the view just by changing lenses—as shown in the three pictures on the right. The girl and the camera stay in the same position for each photograph, showing that subject and background enlarge equally as the angle of view narrows.

1 WIDE ANGLE LENS

The short focal length of a 28mm lens on a 35mm camera means that the angle of view is wide, allowing the whole of the building behind the subject to be photographed. Object size in the viewfinder is small and the foreground prominent.

2 NORMAL LENS

The normal angle of view of a 50mm lens gives a view comparable with your own. Less of the building can be seen as the angle narrows; both the girl and her background have enlarged equally.

3 TELEPHOTO LENS

A 135mm telephoto lens concentrates on the girl. Its long focal length magnifies, but the much narrower angle of view includes less of her surroundings. Compare this picture with the top one: the girl's head is in the same position in relation to the window in the building behind. Both subject and background have grown equally.

1

2

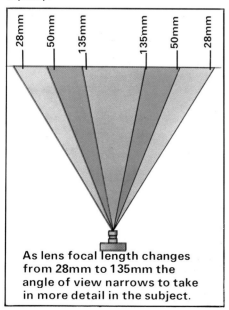

As lens focal length changes from 28mm to 135mm the angle of view narrows to take in more detail in the subject.

3

4

5

6

If, instead of changing the lens, you move the camera to include a different amount of the subject in the viewfinder the angle of view stays the same, but the size of the subject changes in relation to the background. Perspective enlarges objects close to the camera, and is especially noticeable when you photograph a nearby subject with a distant background. If the subject is further away, the effect is less apparent.

The three pictures on the left were all taken using a 50mm lens on an SLR camera. The girl did not move but the camera position was altered. Compare these pictures with the ones opposite; the angle of view has not changed, but the subject gets larger in relation to the background as the camera advances.

4 DISTANCE OF 12m
The building looks tall in relation to the girl; building and subject both appear distant and close together.

5 DISTANCE OF 7·5m
As you move closer to the girl she becomes larger in relation to the background. The feeling of depth in the picture has increased with perspective.

6 DISTANCE OF 2·75m
Here the background is even smaller. The steeper perspective creates the illusion of great distance between the girl and her background. Compare this picture with the one at top to see how the girl's size has altered in relation to hedge, trees and building.

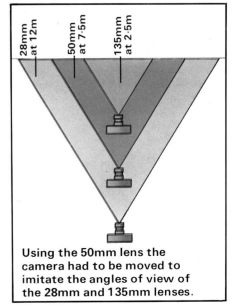

Using the 50mm lens the camera had to be moved to imitate the angles of view of the 28mm and 135mm lenses.

The aperture

When you open the back of a camera to change the film, look inside and then press the shutter release. As the shutter opens the aperture can be seen beyond it. This shows more clearly if you look through the front of the lens or, on a camera with interchangeable lenses, take the lens off and look through that. Turn the aperture control and the size of the aperture will alter within the lens as you change the settings.

As the size of the aperture changes, so does the brightness of the light allowed through the lens. Aperture size, and therefore brightness, is controlled by the iris diaphragm, made up of a number of thin, interleaving blades which rotate to make the aperture larger or smaller. Making it smaller (stopping down the lens) reduces the amount of light reaching the film; increasing the size allows more light through.

The f number system

The brightness of the image on the film depends on the combination of the aperture size (the stop) and the focal length of a lens. So a large aperture and long focal length can transmit the same brightness of light as a small aperture and short focal length.

The scale photographers use to relate focal length and aperture size is called the f number system (f stands for the mathematical term, factor) and it is calculated by measuring the diameter of the aperture and dividing it into the focal length. An aperture of 25mm on a 100mm lens represents f4, but the same diameter aperture on a 50mm lens will represent f2. The smaller the f number, the larger the aperture and, therefore, the more light reaches the film.

The f numbers for any lens are calibrated by the maker on the basis that an aperture of f8, say, will always transmit the same brightness of light whatever the focal length. The series as a whole is arranged so that each f number lets in twice as much light as the number on one side of it and half as much as the number on the other. For example, f4 admits eight times more light than f11, but only half as much as f2·8.

You can see this relationship more easily on the chart on the right. Imagine that f16 allows through half a unit of light: as each f number becomes smaller, so the number of light units doubles.

The size of the aperture affects the image definition of a lens. At maximum aperture the sharpness of the image in

▲ **The iris diaphragm controls the size of the aperture. The thin metal blades rotate with the ring on the lens to make the aperture larger or smaller.**

▼ **Large aperture and long focal length can transmit the same amount of light as a small aperture and short focal length.**
An aperture of the same diameter — say, 25mm — will give a different f number on two lenses of different focal lengths.

the centre of the picture is nearly always greater than in the corners. Stopping down the lens improves central definition slightly and corner definition much more.

Lens construction differs so much that it is impossible to generalize but a sophisticated, large aperture lens of f1·4 probably performs best two or three stops up from its maximum aperture. At small stops such as f16 there is usually slight fall-off in sharpness caused by diffraction, the scattering of light rays collected in the front of the lens as they pass the edge of the iris

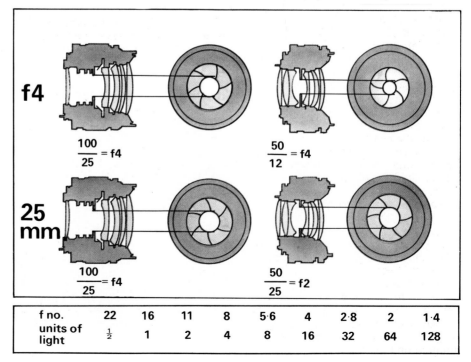

$$\frac{100}{25} = f4 \qquad \frac{50}{12} = f4$$

$$\frac{100}{25} = f4 \qquad \frac{50}{25} = f2$$

f no.	22	16	11	8	5·6	4	2·8	2	1·4
units of light	$\frac{1}{2}$	1	2	4	8	16	32	64	128

▲ The iris diaphragm alters the size of the aperture and therefore the brightness of light reaching the film. Small apertures—f22 and f16—cut down brightness and have great depth of field so all of the picture is sharp. Larger apertures—f11 to f5·6—increase image brightness for normal conditions, while f4 and f2 let in even more light on dull days. Larger apertures have short depths of field decreasing until, at f2, only the subject in focus is completely sharp.

diaphragm. Both these points are really only important when a very high degree of definition is required—such as when copying documents. Other factors, such as camera shake, an incorrectly held camera or incorrect focusing, will have a far more noticeable effect on your pictures.

Depth of field

Depth of field describes the extent of the picture in focus at a given f number. The length of the zone on either side of the subject depends on the size of the aperture and the focal length of the lens. In theory, only the subject on which you focus is completely sharp but an area of acceptable sharpness lies in front of and behind it.

As the size of the aperture decreases, the depth of field lengthens, bringing more of the picture on either side of the subject into focus.

Most rangefinder and reflex cameras have depth of field scales on their lenses, which show the limits of the area in focus for any combination of aperture and distance. A study of this scale shows that the subject focused on is not at the centre of this sharp zone, which extends two-thirds beyond the subject, and one-third towards the camera—unless, of course, the subject is very close to you.

On cameras with separate viewfinders the scale on the lens is the only indication of depth of field, so you should check that the aperture size set will give you the depth you want, before pressing the shutter release.

On SLR cameras, which view through the lens, the photographer can immediately see how much of the finished picture will be in focus by using the depth of field preview button mounted on the camera body.

▲ The atmosphere of the dimly lighted fish market is brought out by using a wide aperture and narrow depth of field to show the patterns made by rows of fish.

▼ The entire cobbled street has photographed sharply using a small aperture. The harsh outlines and narrow shadows are indications of the bright conditions.

▲ The 50mm lens is focused on 2m with an aperture of f1·4, the widest possible setting. The depth of field scale on the lens tells the photographer how much of his subject is in focus (indicated by the shaded area on the lens).

1·40m
2m
3m

▲ The black and white picture shows the positions of the boys in the colour picture. Only the shaded part is in focus. The wide aperture used for this picture gives very short depth of field, extending from immediately in front of the boy with the kite to only about 40cm behind him.

1·40m

2m

3m

▲ The much smaller aperture of f16 used for this second picture has altered the depth of field reading on the lens scale (indicated by the wider shaded area) and includes all objects in the viewfinder between 1·5m and 6m.

With the boys standing in the same positions, the photographer uses a smaller aperture to photograph all three sharply. Again the shaded area denotes depth of field.

Comparing these two pages you can see that depth of field has grown unequally—two thirds beyond the middle child and one third in front.

▲ **24mm lens:** extensive depth of field is characteristic of wide angle lenses—a result of their short focal length. Unless the subject is very close, accurate focusing is not always critical because a large part of the picture will be within the sharp zone (depth of field) of the lens.

▲ **50mm lens:** the longer focal length of this lens shortens depth of field. The distant trees and near end of the bench are out of focus, only the boy and nearby tree are sharp. To give an exact comparison between these different lenses the same aperture, f3·5, is used for the first three illustrations.

Focal length/depth of field

The focal length of the lens on a camera also affects depth of field, as the pictures on this page show. Using the same f number—f4—each time but progressively extending focal length by changing lenses alters the degree of sharpness surrounding the subject in each photograph. So if the same f number is used throughout, depth of field shortens as focal length becomes longer.

To sum up:

● The focal length of a lens determines the angle of view it takes in—that is, the 'width' of the scene.
● Depth of field describes how much of the scene, from front to back, is in focus.
● Depth of field shortens as focal length becomes longer, or as the aperture becomes larger.

Depth of field table

The chart on the right is a rough guide to depth of field at various apertures for each of four lenses, all focused on a subject four metres away. So, depending on the subject and how much of the scene you want to be in focus, you can use this chart to find the right aperture setting for each lens.

The numbers in the boxes give the distance in centimetres that will be in focus (∞ = infinity). For example, 275–765 means that the nearest point in focus is 275cm away from the camera, while the furthest point in focus is 765cm away. Depth of field therefore extends over almost five metres.

Now take, for example, a normal 50mm lens on an SLR camera. Focus on a subject four metres away and look through the camera. Close the aperture progressively from f2·8 to f22. At f4 everything just over three metres to just over six metres will be sharp. At f11 everything from two metres to infinity will be sharp.

Reading down the columns, note how depth of field increases as the aperture becomes smaller—represented by a larger value f number.

Reading across, depth of field for a given aperture decreases as the lens is exchanged for one of longer focal length.

The colour coded diagonals pick out some of the constant depths of field: this way you can choose the right aperture to maintain the same depth of field with different lenses.

DEPTH OF FIELD EXTENDS FOR . . .

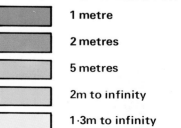

1 metre

2 metres

5 metres

2m to infinity

1·3m to infinity

▲ **135mm lens:** though taken from the same position as with the other two lenses, the telephoto picks out a smaller area of the view. Compared with a 24mm lens depth of field is minimal and focusing is therefore critical. Only a very small part of the picture is sharp.

▲ **135mm lens:** to show that depth of field can be increased dramatically with the use of a smaller aperture, this photograph was taken with the same 135mm lens but set at f22. Changing to a small aperture brings the tree and bench into sharp focus.

DEPTH OF FIELD TABLE (IN CENTIMETRES)

f no.		25mm lens	50mm lens	100mm lens	200mm lens
2·8	⬤	275—765	325—525	355—455	375—425
4	⬤	240—1430	310—610	340—480	360—450
5·6	⬤	200—∞	275—765	325—525	355—455
8	⬤	170—∞	240—1430	310—610	340—480
11	⬤	130—∞	200—∞	275—765	325—525
16	⬤	110—∞	170—∞	240—1430	310—610
22	⬤	80—∞	130—∞	200—∞	275—765

∞ = infinity

The shutter

Early cameras had no shutters as we know them today. Films were so slow and exposures so long that the photographer simply removed the lens cap, then replaced it at the end of the exposure time. But, as film emulsions became more sensitive, a device was needed to control the length of time the light was allowed to fall on the film. Today's shutter can give accurate exposures as short as 1/2000 of a second.

The range of shutter speeds on a camera are similar to the aperture's f numbers in that each speed either doubles or halves the one next to it. A range, which is calibrated in fractions of a second, will usually read: 1/1000, 1/500, 1/250, 1/125, 1/60, 1/30, 1/15, 1/8 1/4, 1/2, 1, and B. B stands for Brief time and is used for longer, manually timed exposures, because the shutter stays open as long as the release is pressed open. This makes it possible to take night-time photographs and interiors without using additional lighting. All modern cameras, apart from large format types, have a dual-purpose film advance lever, tensioning the shutter at the same time as the film is wound on. This saves time between exposures and prevents the possibility of accidental multiple exposures.

Shutter types

Basically, there are two main types of shutter: those that work inside or just behind the lens, known as between lens shutters, including sector shutters; and focal plane shutters, which are positioned close to the film.

Between lens shutters

The between lens shutter closely resembles the aperture and is positioned between the lens elements, near the aperture blades. It is made up of a number of thin, overlapping metal blades, which spring open for the time of the exposure and then close again. As the blades start to open, a small star-shaped hole appears in the centre of the shutter and grows during the exposure. It is very light and compact, and can synchronize with flash at all speeds. But between lens shutters have two drawbacks: few work at speeds of over 1/500, and they are costly to produce for cameras with interchangeable lenses. This is because each lens requires its own integral shutter and a separate means to block light from the film when the lens is removed.

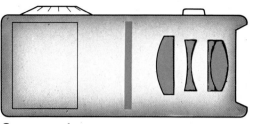

Sector shutters

The sector shutter is used on many cameras with small diameter lenses, such as the pocket 110 and simple viewfinder cameras. It is mounted just behind the lens, and consists of a spring-loaded metal plate which prevents light reaching the film until the shutter release is pressed. There is usually a choice of two speeds, indicated by weather symbols marked on the outside of the camera. The faster speed is used in bright, sunny conditions and the slower one on cloudy days. Some cameras also have a separate setting for flash attachments.

▲ Between lens 'leaf-type' shutter showing opening sequence.

◄ The section through a 110 camera shows the sector shutter, coloured red, lying just behind the lens.

▼ A typical sector shutter. When the shutter release is pressed the plate springs back momentarily to let the light reach the film.

► On a between lens shutter, as the shutter release is pressed, lever A cocks the mechanism and lever B triggers the exposure.

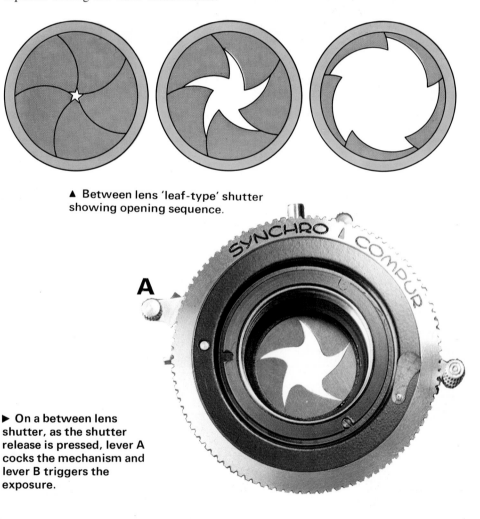

Focal plane shutters

Focal plane shutters are made up of two blinds positioned just in front of the film, with an adjustable gap between them, which follow each other across the film plane. High speeds (up to 1/2000) are obtained by altering the size of the gap between the blinds, and lower speeds (down to 1 second) by holding back the second blind after the first has travelled across.

The majority of focal plane shutters are made from rubberized cloth and move horizontally across the film, but they will only permit flash synchronization on speeds up to 1/60. A growing minority use metal bladed shutters which travel vertically, and can synchronize with flash at speeds to 1/125, because of the shorter distance the shutter has to cover in a 35mm camera. As a focal plane shutter is mounted inside the camera body, close to the film, it protects the film from light when the lens is changed. Extra lenses do not need their own built-in shutter.

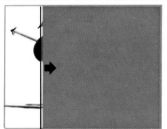   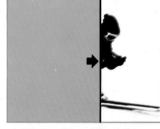

▲ As soon as the shutter release is pressed the first blind starts to move across. Light can reach the first section of film and begin the exposure.

▲ The gap between the blinds passes across the film. The width of the gap depends on the shutter speed, so the second blind may now start to cross.

▲ The second blind continues its passage across the film, completing the exposure on the first part of the frame. The leading blind has almost finished its crossing.

▲ The trailing blind completes the exposure, making sure that the entire frame receives an equal amount of light. When it has crossed, light is again blocked.

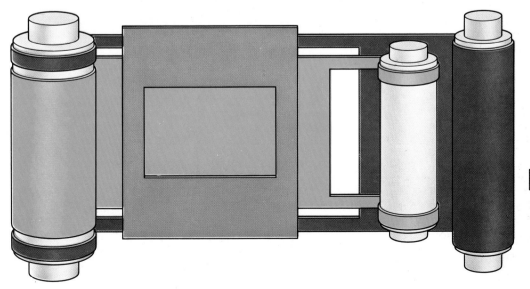

◄ As the film is wound on for the next exposure the shutter blinds are tensioned and light is blocked from the film.

▼ The focal plane shutter is mounted immediately in front of the film.

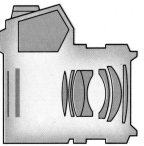

Stopping movement

The shutter can also be used to express movement in different ways. A fast shutter speed will stop or freeze movement and a slow one will register a blurred image of a moving subject.

The very short exposure time of a high shutter speed can freeze movement and give a sharp image of a moving subject. The speed needed to stop this movement depends on three things: the speed of the moving subject, the distance between the camera and the subject, and the angle at which it is travelling towards the camera.

The closer the subject is, the higher the shutter speed must be. But a great deal depends on the direction of the movement—something travelling towards the camera photographs more sharply at a lower speed than something moving across the camera's field of view. As a rough guide, in normal conditions objects moving towards the camera photograph sharply at 1/125; at an oblique angle of, say, 45°, at 1/250; and if they are travelling parallel to the camera, at 1/500.

Expressing movement

But the photographer will not always want to 'stop' the movement of the subject. A racing car, a running child or someone on a bicycle all involve movement—and the camera can be used to express this.

You can convey the feeling of movement by using a slow shutter speed. However, take care to avoid blurring the whole picture, which can happen with too slow a shutter speed, and resulting camera shake. The background needs to stay sharp to keep the feeling of movement. A trial-and-error guide is to estimate the shutter speed necessary to stop the subject completely and then use the speed one setting slower.

▼ In the pictures below and right the shutter speed on the camera has been increased from 1/15 to 1/60 and 1/250. At 1/15 the motorbike travelling towards the camera is slightly blurred, but as it crosses in front of the camera it is almost unrecognizable.
At 1/60 the lower picture is sharp but the bike travelling across is quite blurred.

At 1/250 the much faster speed just stops the motion of the cyclist.
It would have been even sharper if a speed of 1/500 had been used.
Picture A, also taken at 1/60, shows the motor-cyclist travelling at an oblique angle to the camera.
Compare the blur in this picture with the two taken at 1/60 to see how blur increases as the angle of the subject changes.

A

SPEEDS TO STOP MOVEMENT			
Camera to subject distances	Movement towards	Movement at 45°	Movement across
slow subjects: 5 metres under 5 mph: 10 metres 20 metres	1/60 1/30 1/15	1/125 1/60 1/30	1/250 1/125 1/60
faster subjects: 10 metres 20 metres 30 metres	1/250 1/125 1/60	1/500 1/250 1/125	1/1000 1/500 1/250

▼ Using a slow shutter speed is often an extremely effective way to express movement in a subject. Enough of the picture must be sharp to tell a story, but the photographer has caught the gay mood of the two Indian girls on a swing by emphasizing the flow of their movement.

Camera shake

The speeds most often used by photographers are 1/125 and 1/250, but 1/60 and lower can be used if you avoid camera shake. If the camera moves, even slightly, while the shutter is being released the edges of an otherwise sharp picture will be blurred. Longer focal length lenses accentuate any camera movement so, if you can hold the camera still at 1/60 with a 50mm lens, you should increase this to 1/125 for a 105mm lens. On a 28mm wide angle lens the shutter speed can be as slow as 1/30 without loss of sharpness.

Panning the camera

One of the ways often used to express movement is to pan the camera. This has the effect of keeping the moving subject sharp while blurring the background, giving subject detail plus a strong feeling of speed and motion. To do this the camera follows the path of the subject, keeping pace with its movement. It takes practice and a steady hand.

Stand with your feet apart facing the spot where you intend to take the picture. Without moving your feet, centre the subject in the viewfinder and, as it moves towards you, follow its movement smoothly swinging from the hips. When the subject is directly in front of you, press the shutter but continue to follow through the movement to avoid any possibility of jerking

1 f2·8 1/500

EXAMPLES OF EXPOSURE SPEEDS

The larger the f number the greater the depth of field but the slower the shutter speed for given exposure.

Limited depth of field					Large depth of field	
f2	f2.8	f4	f5.6	f8	f11	f16
1/1000	1/500	1/250	1/125	1/60	1/30	1/15
Movement stopped					Movement recorded blurred	

the camera. Try using 1/60 or even 1/30—once the technique is mastered you can use very slow shutter speeds to increase the degree of background blur.

Obviously, you can achieve varying degrees of sharpness and blur by using a range of shutter speeds and these techniques. These combinations can, for instance, blur the feet and arms of a sprinter but register the agony of exhaustion on his face.

Shutter and aperture

Both shutter and aperture control the amount of light reaching the film, but their effects are quite different. The size of the aperture controls the depth of field—how much of the picture will be sharp—while the shutter speed dictates how sharp a moving subject

will be. Correct exposure is a combination of shutter speed and aperture setting, but the photographer can select any combination of these settings that adds up to the correct amount of light. For example, if the correct exposure for the photograph of the child is 1/125 at f5·6, the negative will be correctly exposed at either 1/500 at f2·8, or 1/15 at f16. But both these combinations have certain limitations. The photographer nearly always has to choose between a fast shutter speed to stop a certain movement or a small aperture to give a sharp result from 5m to infinity.

Both combinations can give the correct exposure but produce different pictures. Sometimes it is possible to achieve both a small f stop and high shutter speed in very bright conditions.

▼ These pictures illustrate the shutter/aperture combination.

1 A high shutter speed freezes the girl skipping, but the wide aperture needed for a correct exposure shortens depth of field, putting the trees out of focus.

2 A medium speed cannot stop the faster movement of the girl's hands and feet although her body is sharp. The medium aperture gives greater depth of field, with the background in focus.

3 A slow shutter speed blurs the subject entirely, but the complementary small aperture extends depth of field beyond the evergreen tree in the distance.

2 f5·6   1/125

3 f16   1/15

Getting the exposure right

Choosing the best exposure for a picture is just as important as getting the image sharp. A beautiful holiday picture on the beach is spoiled if you cannot see details of the people in the photographs—they may be too light or dark.

A correctly exposed negative or slide will have a full range of tones from deep shadows to bright highlights. Under-expose your photograph and the darker parts of the picture will contain little detail; over-expose, and the bright parts will appear all washed out and lacking in detail.

Guessing the exposure (based on the film manufacturer's guide sheet in every film pack) may be successful on a reasonably bright day when there are no deep shadows or patches of very strong sunlight. But the more extreme the lighting conditions become, the more difficult it is to guess accurately.

Types of meter

An exposure meter measures the brightness of the subject and, based on the speed of the film you are using, gives you a guide to the f number and shutter speed to use. Most 35mm cameras, especially SLRs, and even some 110 cameras, now have built-in exposure meters. Some work automatically and set the camera's controls for you, but with others you have to adjust either the shutter speed or the aperture manually. Hand-held exposure meters are still used too, mainly for special situations like low light or night photography, and for incident light readings (see overleaf).

Both hand-held and built-in exposure meters contain a photo-electric cell which measures the amount of light falling on it. There are three types of cell.

Selenium cell: too large for most built-in meters, a selenium cell powers itself. It needs no batteries. Any light which reaches the cell generates a small electric current which is measured by a galvanometer needle along a scale. Used mainly in hand-held meters, this type doesn't respond well in very low light.

The CdS cell: the development of a tiny, sensitive cell using cadmium sulphide made built-in meters possible for the vast majority of 35mm cameras. It can give readings even in moonlight, but takes a little time to settle down if you move quickly from bright sunshine to dark shade.

Silicon cell: the newest meters use a miniature silicon cell. This is very accurate and adjusts quickly to changing light conditions. It can cope with any contrast, from the brightest sun to night-time. Miniaturization has made this cell so small that, even with an amplifier and batteries, it can be fitted into a 110 camera.

Through the lens metering

The majority of SLR cameras have built-in meters which measure the light entering the lens. The meter often has the same angle of view as the lens on the camera so measures light over a wider area for a wide angle lens, and over a narrower area for a telephoto. Some TTL meters take an average reading from the total amount of light entering the lens, not differentiating between bright areas of sky and the darker land. Others, which are more accurate, also measure the light as a central spot (perhaps one-fifth of the total picture area). The best alternative is probably to use a third system—centre-weighted. This gives preference to the light reading at the centre of the picture using one cell, but co-ordinates with a second cell which takes the rest of the frame area into account.

Exposure information collected by the metering system is usually displayed in the viewfinder in one of two ways: either by a needle which moves between two markers or by LEDs (small bright lights) which are colour coded for correct over- or under-exposure. These lights are less easily affected by rough handling than the older, needle systems, but use up battery power much faster.

Automatic metering

An increasing number of SLR and viewfinder cameras with meters are semi or fully automatic. The latter select the correct exposure combination without the photographer's help. But there are two types of semi-automatic cameras; those which select a shutter speed to match the f number chosen by the photographer (aperture priority) and those which select the right aperture to suit a manually set shutter speed (shutter priority).

Aperture priority suits still subjects, landscapes and pictures in which depth of field is important.

HAND-HELD METERS
Three types of hand-held meter with different qualities: the Weston Euro-Master relies on a solar powered selenium cell which produces a current from the light reaching it, and requires no batteries. The Gossen Profisix needs batteries for its highly sensitive silicon cell, and accepts attachments to read in moonlight, by flash or in the darkroom for working out enlarger exposures. The Minolta Spotmeter II also uses batteries, which power a computer able to work out the average of two 17 spot readings or calculate highlight and shadow exposures.

Average reading: two photo-electric cells receive light from the lens via the pentaprism, and average it across its entire area. The result can be misleading unless the subject is fairly evenly lit, but a simple solution is to take the reading close by the subject.

Spot reading: this type of meter is very precise, but harder to use. Only light at the centre of the lens is measured so, for overall views, choose a mid-tone as representative and line it up in the centre of the lens. Alternatively, take several readings and average them.

Centre-weighted reading: this is probably the easiest type of TTL meter to use. The meter takes the whole area viewed by the lens into account but gives more importance to the central area. Be careful if your main point of interest is not, in fact, at the centre of the picture.

Shutter priority has the advantage when photographing moving subjects, because you choose the shutter speed. Stopping movement is more important than depth of field.

A few of the more expensive cameras, like the Canon A-1, have a choice of priorities, including fully automatic exposure control which requires no manual setting of aperture or shutter speed. You can move from one to the other or take full manual control at the flick of a lever.

Integral exposure meters

Some viewfinder cameras also have integral exposure meters. These do not meter through the lens, but use a cell mounted either next to the viewfinder window or surrounding the lens (Olympus Trip 35). They are usually coupled to the aperture/shutter mechanism in the same way as SLR cameras, although most are fully automatic. With other models, you simply align a needle or see a light that indicates the correct exposure.

Taking a reading

You can measure the light either from the camera position or from close to the subject. The reading can be taken in two ways: using the light reflected from the subject or the incident light falling on the subject. Incident light readings can only be taken using a hand-held meter.

A reflected light reading, taken by both built-in and hand-held meters, measures the light bouncing off the subject. It can be measured either from

USING A HAND-HELD METER
Hand-held meters usually have two scales, with different numeric values, one for high-intensity, the other for low-intensity light. The photographer transfers the value recorded on the scale to the calculator dial by hand: this sets a full range of aperture/ shutter speed combinations.

— LIGHT READING SCALE
— GALVONOMETER NEEDLE
— CALCULATOR
— NEEDLE RELEASE SWITCH
— SHUTTER SPEED SCALE
— FILM SPEED SETTING
— APERTURE SETTING

▲ To take a reflected light reading point the meter's cell at the subject. Do not cover the cell with your hand. It can be taken at either subject or camera position.

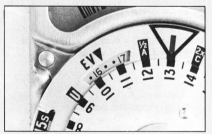

1 It is important to set the speed (ASA) of the film in your camera on the meter before taking a reading.

2 Point the cell on the meter where you wish to take a reading, releasing the needle release switch with your thumb.

3 Find the value of the reading on the dial and move the aperture setting scale until the pointer lines up with the right number.

4 Several exposure combinations of shutter speed and aperture are now lined up on the dial. Choose one appropriate to your subject.

▲ To take an incident light reading from the subject cover the cell on the meter with its dome and point the cell towards the camera.

the camera position, where you will actually take the photograph, or close to the subject. Taking the reading from the camera position will give an overall impression of the available light, including the background. But, if one part of the picture is more important than the rest, walk up to it and take the reading, or measure the light on a substitute. For example, a hand held close to the meter will represent skin tones in a portrait if similarly lit.

An incident light reading measures the intensity of the light falling on the subject. You need a hand-held meter with a translucent dome or Invercone covering the cell in order to do this. The reading is taken close to the subject with the meter and incident light dome pointing towards the camera. It is a more accurate way to measure the exposure for a subject with a broad range of tones and ensures properly exposed highlights. To use an exposure meter in this way takes a little longer and so works best with a static subject, but the result is a correct exposure in a difficult situation.

TTL meters are quicker to use than a hand-held meter. Simply line up the needle in the viewfinder between its over- and under-exposure markers by altering the aperture or shutter speed. Several combinations of aperture and shutter speed will make the needle line up, or the correct LED shine, and it is up to you to choose the best combination. Avoid shutter speeds less than 1/60 unless using a support.

Estimating the exposure outdoors without a meter is not impossible. The following suggestions will give reasonably accurate results, provided you choose uncomplicated situations with fairly even lighting.

• Match the shutter speed as closely as possible to the speed (ASA) of the film in the camera.

• Presuming that the sun is more or less behind the camera, the correct f number will be:

Bright summer sunlight	f16
Hazy sunlight	f11
Bright, cloudy days	f8
Overcast sky or shade	f5·6

• To avoid over-exposure of a subject which is fairly light in tone and lit by strong, direct sunlight, use f22.

These combinations will be accurate to within half an f stop. But, provided you keep the total exposure constant, there is no reason why you should not change a setting of 1/125 at f16 to one of 1/250 at f11 for a moving subject.

▲ These two pictures represent situations where a general overall reading will give good results. The lighting is fairly even, the small area of deep shadow under the bridge and the highlight on the parapet are both too small to affect the exposure. In the lower picture the area of bright yellow flowers equals the area of dark stalks.

The exposure guide in the film pack and our suggestions for estimating exposure should give similar results with or without a meter.

▼ Bracketing exposures: to be sure of a correct result take two more (identical) pictures using one click stop or shutter speed setting over or under the original setting.

Wide angle lenses

If you do not yet own a wide angle lens, you are probably thinking of buying one. Nowadays, there is a huge range of wide angles on the market, and it can be difficult trying to decide which to get. Not only are you faced with a choice of focal lengths, you must also decide whether to buy your camera maker's own lens or an independent make, and what size maximum aperture to go for.

However, the decision is not as daunting as it looks.

Why buy a wide?

A wide angle lens is one that has a shorter focal length than a standard lens. As a rule, anything with a focal length of 35mm or less qualifies as wide angle.

The great advantage of these lenses is that they let you take in much more of a scene from the same viewpoint than a standard lens does. This makes them especially useful for taking photographs in confined spaces. This includes, indoors, in a crowded market place or for photographing buildings across the street. They are also ideal for landscape photography.

Which focal length?

The first thing to decide is what focal length to get. The most common focal lengths that you have to choose from are the 35mm, 28mm and 24mm. There are a number of lenses with focal lengths less than 24mm, but these are extreme wide angle lenses that are used for special effect shots rather than normal, everyday photogrpahy.

The 35mm lens gives you about 50 per cent more view than a standard 50mm lens. Quite often, this is not enough where the subject is large or you cannot get far enough away. Because of this, the 35mm is often regarded nowadays as being more of a standard lens than a wide angle. In fact, some SLRs now come with 40mm standard lens, and 38mm is common on compact cameras. Most people who already own a 50mm lens feel that there is not enough difference between it and a 35mm lens to warrant buying one.

At the more extreme end, a 24mm lens gives you over twice the angle of view of a 50mm lens. But it does impose a steep perspective on the scene, and almost invariably makes the resulting composition like a wide angle picture. This can be very effective with some shots, but you may not want a steep perspective every time you use a wide angle lens.

A typical selection of 28mm lenses: (1) Mamiya Sekor E f3·5, (2) Makinon f2·8, an independent lens, (3) Nikon Series E f2·8, (4) Zuiko f3·5 for Olympus OM.

In between these two is the 28mm lens. This lets you get in much closer to a scene than a 35mm lens, yet its perspective is not so steep that it is forever reminding you that it's a wide angle. It is the shortest focal length lens that produces 'normal' looking pictures, when required. Yet it will still give you a strong perspective when you want it to create a special effect.

Which make?

Most 28mm lenses (apart from the very cheapest) give excellent quality pictures. As far as results go, there's very little to choose between the camera maker's own lens and the well-known independent makes such as Vivitar, Tamron and Hoya. However, there are some points worth bearing in mind when you decide on which make to buy.

50mm ANGLE OF VIEW
▲ ▶ A 50mm standard lens gives you an angle of view of 46° from corner to corner on 35mm film. This angle increases or decreases in proportion to the focal length of a lens.

28mm ANGLE OF VIEW
▲ ▶ A 28mm lens takes in a much wider angle of view than a 50mm lens — 75°. Subjects the same distance away appear almost half the size they do through a 50mm lens.

If you stick to the camera maker's lens, then you can be sure that the colour balance and contrast, and the optical quality of your pictures will be the same as that given by your standard lens. The aperture and focusing rings will be identical, which is an advantage for ease of use and rapid picture taking. Also the filter thread sizes will very likely be the same—so you won't need to buy new filters.

With independent lenses, all these factors may be different, and it will certainly have different control rings. On the other hand, it will most likely be cheaper than the maker's own. The reason for this is that independent lenses are made to fit a wide range of camera makes whereas Canon lenses, say, only fit Canon cameras. So the sales of independent lenses may be greater, which allows the manufacturer to lower the price of each lens.

If an independent lens is more than a third cheaper than the maker's own, then it is probably of cheaper construction. But you may still be quite happy with it if you don't intend to use it very often.

All maker's own lenses and most independents have fixed mounts, which means that a particular lens can only be fitted to one make of camera. But there are a few independent lens manufacturers who make lenses with interchangeable mounts—the Tamron Adaptall-2 range is an example. If you change your camera brand, you only need to buy a new mount for your lens.

Which aperture?

Having made up your mind about which make to get, you then have to decide on what size maximum aperture you need and can afford.

Normal 28mm lenses have a maximum aperture of f2·8, or occasionally f3·5. There are also faster types—f2 or f1·8, and even the ultra-fast f1·4 or less. The ultra-fast wide angles are specialist lenses and much too expensive to be considered as your first wide angle lens. The choice is between buying the normal f2·8 and paying the extra for the additional stop that you get with the faster f2 lens.

With a 28mm lens, you can safely take hand-held shots at a shutter speed one step slower than you can with a standard lens. So if you take sharp pictures at 1/60 with a 50mm lens, you will be able to take sharp pictures with a 28mm lens at 1/30. Having a lens one stop slower than your standard (which is probably about f2) is thus no great disadvantage, since you can hand-hold it at slower speeds.

The 28mm f2·8 is often a fine lens optically. It should be almost the same size

▲ Viewed through a 50mm lens, the perspective of a scene is much the same as that seen by our eyes (left). With a 28mm lens, you have to move in nearly twice as close to the subject to regain its original size on the film (right).

This gives the picture an exaggerated perspective. It is not caused by the lens being wide angle, as many people think, but by your adopting a viewpoint closer to the subject. The persective is unusual but not unnatural.

▼ ▶ Modern 28mm lenses are compact and light. This Nikon Series E f2·8 lens, reproduced here slightly larger than life-size, weighs only 5·4oz (150g) and is 1·8in (44mm) long.

as your standard lens and so will fit easily into your camera case. An f2, on the other hand, will probably be bigger, weigh more, and will certainly cost more. It may need larger filters, and it may not give you such good pictures. Its most likely faults are distortions, so that straight lines are rendered as slight curves, and a decrease in edge sharpness and contrast.

Therefore unless you often take pictures at low light levels, such as indoors, it is best to go for the f2·8.

Closest focusing distance

Lenses usually differ slightly in their specifications. You will find it useful if the lens you choose has a fairly short closest focusing distance since you cannot use extension tubes with it. (Even the shortest tube makes a 28mm lens focus only a few inches away.) The closest focusing distance should be about 8in-12in (20cm-30cm). For wide angle effects it is often very important to have sharp detail close to the camera. If the lens does not focus this close, or at least to 18in, (45cm) you may eventually find it limiting.

Lens hoods

It is well worth while buying a lens hood for your 28mm. It cuts out a lot of flare and thus increases the contrast of your pictures. Do not use your standard lens hood on it, though—it is the wrong shape and will cut off the corners of your pictures. Buy a special wide angle lens hood. These are worth while for all makes of lenses.

Wide angle zooms

There is a large range of wide angle zoom lenses on the market that include the 28mm focal length. Most firms now offer a 24-48 or 28-50mm zoom or similar lens that can be bought instead of the 50mm standard. If you buy one of these instead of separate fixed length lenses, then you will have all focal lengths from 24 or 28mm up to 50mm. However, they are much bigger and heavier, more expensive, and the maximum aperture is limited fo f3·5 or more. Also their optical quality is rarely as good as a fixed length 50mm standard or 28mm lens.

While these lenses are ideal for snapshot and holiday photography, they are not really a substitute for a 28mm fixed focal length lens.

Perspective and distortion

People often say that a wide angle lens distorts perspective. This is not true.

▲ In confined spaces, a 28mm lens still allows a reasonable view of a scene. Notice the enhanced sense of depth given by wide angle lenses. *John Garrett*

Because they cover such a wide area you have to get closer in to your subject than you would with a standard lens. This makes nearby objects look much larger than more distant objects, but it is a true rendering, not a distortion. (The perspective changes because of the change of viewpoint, not the focal length.)

With a 28mm lens, you do get some distortion, but this happens only at the edges of the picture. If you photograph a group of people that fills the frame, then the heads of the outermost figures will look slightly elongated. But commercially produced prints and transparencies are always cropped, and you usually lose the distorted parts of the picture.

Nevertheless, if you want 'normal-looking' pictures for your 28mm lens, make sure that your subject is positioned centrally with plenty of space between it and the edges of the picture. Avoid shooting people from extreme angles and from close in—unless doing it for effect.

If you want to use the wide angle effect creatively, then the 28mm lens lets you do so. Shoot from very close in, use extreme angles and fill your frame with the subject. The impact will make you glad you decided to invest in a wide angle.

Telephoto lenses

When you come to buy your first telephoto lens, you may well be put off by the huge range that confronts you: fixed focal length lenses in a wide variety. . . macro. . . zooms which cover the telephoto range.

Every one has its uses, depending on the kind of pictures you like to take. One day, you may own several. But for your *'first'* telephoto lens, your best bet is to buy 135mm.

Why buy a telephoto?

A telephoto lens is one that has a longer focal length than a standard lens. It gives you a smaller angle of view and a greater magnification than a standard, which makes it ideal for photographing subjects at a distance. It is ideal at events where you are often not allowed to get closer to the action. It is also ideal when photographing wildlife, without disturbing the subject.

It is also the natural lens to use for portrait work since it lets you take head-and-shoulder shots without being too close to the subject, and its flatter perspective (compared to a standard lens used closer to the subject) gives a pleasing result.

The choice facing you

When you buy a telephoto, the first thing you have to decide is whether to buy a fixed focal length lens or whether to buy a zoom lens.

Telephoto zoom lenses are available in a variety of ranges, such as 70-150mm and 80-200mm. Their standard of performance is increasing all the time, but they still do not give quite the quality picture that you can get from a fixed lens. They may also cost twice as much as a 135mm lens and are twice as heavy—an important consideration when you come to take hand-held shots.

Among the fixed length lenses, anything with a focal length of over 200mm is really a specialist lens for wildlife or sports enthusiasts. They are expensive and heavy, and need a tripod for truly sharp pictures. So the choice is between telephoto lenses with a focal length of 200mm or less, and the cheapest of these lenses, in any manufacturer's range, is generally the 135mm.

135mm lenses

All manufacturers making lenses for 35mm cameras include a 135mm lens in their range. These lenses are made in great numbers—far more than any other size of telephoto.

▲ Here are some typical 135mm lenses. (1) Makinon f2·8, which has a special close-focusing ring allowing a reproduction of 1:4·5; (2) Zuiko f2·8 for Olympus cameras; (3) Nikkor f2·8; (4) Nikkor f3·5, less than one stop slower than the f2·8 but cheaper and lighter, and (5) Mamiya-Sekor E f3·5.

This has two advantages: it makes them cheaper than any other size, and many manufacturers have put a lot of research into the design of these lenses to ensure good performance. Research has in turn led to some very compact, light 135mm lenses being designed. It has also allowed them to be built with reasonably large maximum apertures, such as f2·8. Typically, a modern 135mm lens weighs 11oz-14oz (300g-400g) and is only 3in-4in (75mm-100mm) long.

These lenses give you a field of view of roughly 18°. It is the longest focal length at which you can take head-and-shoulders portraits in an average room. yet the magnification is sufficient to pull in distant objects to a reasonable size on the film.

Which make?

You can either buy a 135mm lens made by your own camera manufacturer, or you can buy one made by an independent lens manufacturer, such as Vivitar, Tamron or Hoya. All 135mm lenses except the very cheapest give good results, but there are some differences worth bearing in mind between the maker's own lens and the independents.

If you buy the camera maker's own lens, then its colour rendition should be exactly the same as that of your standard lens. (Every lens has an effect—however slight—on the colour balance of the light passing through it.) The 135mm will also have the same controls and handling, and will very likely take the same size filters. On the other hand, independent lenses are cheaper. The reason is that they are made to fit most popular camera mounts whereas camera makers' lenses only fit their own mount. So many more independent lenses may be sold than any particular camera maker's lens.

Also, the optical quality of an independent may be lower.

Which aperture?

Many makers offer a choice of maximum aperture, typically f3·5 and f2·8. The difference in speed may be less than one stop, as with the example quoted here, but there are other important

50mm ANGLE OF VIEW
▲ ▶ A 50mm standard lens gives you an angle of view of 46° across the diagonal of a frame. This can be too large if the subject is distant and inaccessible, as it is here.

135mm ANGLE OF VIEW
▲ ▶ A 135mm lens takes in an angle of 18°— equivalent to a magnification of 2.7 times that of a standard lens. With it, you can often fill the frame even with inaccessible subjects.

differences.

The faster lens will certainly be more expensive, and it will probably be better optically. Also, it provides a slightly brighter viewfinder image for framing and focusing. Against this, the f3·5 lens will be smaller and lighter, and is more likely to take the same filter thread size as your standard lens. The weight of the f3·5 lens makes it easier to hand hold. This is an important factor, as magnifying the image also magnifies the effect of camera shake. Thus while you may be able to hand-hold an f3·5 lens satisfactorily, at a shutter speed of 1/125, it will be harder to do this with the faster, heavier lens.

If you intend to use the f2·8 lens a lot at full aperture, for shooting candids or floodlit sports, say, then the faster lens will certainly be useful. Otherwise, you may find the slower lens much better value.

These lenses are heavy—the Nikkor weighs 30oz (860g)—and very expensive. Their quality is high, but unless you often need to shoot at f2, the sheer bulk of these lenses makes them impractical for general use.

Teleconverters

If you think that a 135mm lens is not nearly powerful enough for your first telephoto, think about teleconverters. These give much better results with telephoto lenses, and most cheap teleconverters are designed to match 135mm lenses best.

With a 2x teleconverter, a 135mm f2·8 lens becomes a 270mm f5·6. A 3x teleconverter makes it into a 400mm f8. This may seem a little slow, but it is not far off a typical 400mm f6·3 lens. Teleconverters introduce some pincushion distortion, to which 135mm lenses are prone anyway. The combined

effects of a poor 135mm lens and a poor teleconverter may produce unacceptably bad pictures, so choose your teleconverter carefully.

A good teleconverter can be really useful, and using a 2x with a 135mm is an economical way to find out if you *really* need a 300mm 'long tom'. However, remember that a 300mm is much less convenient to carry around than a tiny teleconverter.

Special features

Its worth bearing in mind when you come to choose a lens, that different 135mm lenses may offer different features.

Close focus and macro lenses. Some 135mm lenses have a second focusing ring that moves the front lens elements further out to allow close focusing. They can give a magnification of up to half lifesize, though the image quality may be poor.

50mm PERSPECTIVE
▲ The perspective given by a 50mm lens on 35mm film is roughly the same as that seen by your eye.

135mm PERSPECTIVE
▲ Because a 135mm lens gives a magnified image, it is used from further away and the perspective appears flattened.

Modern 135mm lenses are compact and light. This Nikkor f3·5, reproduced here slightly larger than life-size, takes the same filter size (52mm) as Nikon's standard lenses. It weighs just 14oz (400g) and is 3.5in (9cm) long.

True macro 135mm lenses, specially designed for close up work and giving life-size reproduction, are also available. They are very expensive but their quality is excellent.

Minimum focusing distance. This may be as close as 4ft (1.3m) or less on a good lens. Cheaper ones may not focus closer than 6ft (2m). A close-focusing 135mm is ideal for hand-held close-ups, as you can fill the frame from further away than with a standard lens.

Small minimum aperture. Quite a few 135mm lenses have a minimum aperture of f32. You will need a tripod at this aperture, but it can be very useful for extra depth of field for landscape subjects and still life pictures. Some lenses offer f64. However, bear in mind that lens performance falls off at these small apertures.

Built-in lens hoods. Nearly all 135mm lenses have built-in lens hoods that slide forward over the front of the lens. They help to reduce flare and thus increase contrast. If the lens does not have a built-in hood, buy one specially designed for this focal length.

▲ Because of its longer focal length, a 135mm lens has a shallower depth of field. *Robin Bath*

▼ The same lens as left, here on a Nikon EM. The combination is easily hand held.

Zoom lenses

You are standing in the middle of a crowd, photographing a football match. With your 100mm telephoto lens the players look far too small when the action moves to the far goal mouth, but if you fit your 200mm telephoto lens you get cut-off heads and feet when players move near you.

You are standing on the edge of a harbour wall, photographing a lighthouse. You want it to fill the frame precisely, with no wasted space. Neither your 135mm nor your 200mm allows this—you need 163mm. If you could move in closer or move back, your problems would be solved—but you can't . . .

You are climbing a mountain, and don't want to be weighed down with equipment. Nor do you want to be changing lenses, as this occupies your hands, which are better used for climbing. But you want a wide angle lens for close-ups of your fellow climbers and a medium telephoto for views of the scenery.

These three problems have the same answer—the zoom lens. Zoom lenses have been called '100 focal lengths in one lens'—instead of producing a fixed image, they can 'zoom' in to magnify the image, or zoom back to get more in the frame. Zoom lenses were first introduced on cine cameras but are now almost universal on stills cameras, especially on 35mm SLRs.

Making a zoom lens is a fairly complex operation, though the principle is simple. If you change the separation between two elements (or groups) in a photographic lens, you change the focal length of the combination. But you also change other things like the distance of the film from the lens, and the f stop.

Modern zoom lenses use anything from nine to 18 glass elements, moving apart or closer together in tracks worked out by computer to change focal lengths without altering accurate focus settings or the f stop. In addition, all the usual aberrations and distortions which even normal standard lenses can have, must be eliminated as far as possible.

Cheap zooms tend to be optically compensated—that is, by careful optical design a relatively simple movement of one group in the lens does everything, zooming perfectly and holding sharp focus. But to achieve this, the lens may be bulky, have a limited aperture or poor performance.

The more expensive zoom lenses are usually mechanically compensated, with tracks allowing two or three groups to move in different directions as the lens is zoomed.

100-300mm

80-210mm

75-150mm

28-80mm

21-35mm

85-210mm

Zooms can cover an enormous range of focal lengths. A single lens may run from 35-200mm, and if used with a 21-35mm would cover in two lenses an outfit normally composed of at least seven. Popular ranges like 75-150 or 85-210 cover telephoto options; longer versions like 100-300mm appeal to sports and wildlife photographers; mid-range zooms like 35-70mm or 28-80mm are 'one lens outfits' for everyday use.

Most zooms are similar in size to the long focal length on their scale—for example, an 80–210mm zoom resembles a 200mm lens, not an 80mm. Wide angle and mid-range zooms may be even larger, though in the case of some pure wide angle zooms the reverse happens—a 24–50mm zoom is more like a 24mm than a standard 50mm. They are usually one f stop smaller than a normal prime lens of the longest or shortest focal length (80–200mm—f4·5, as opposed to 200mm—f3·5; 24–50mm—f4, as opposed to 24mm—f2·8). Regardless of size, most zooms are heavy because of the amount of glass and metal used.

Choosing a lens

To choose the kind of zoom you need, bear in mind your kind of photography.
● The family photographer needs a mid-range 35–80mm, ideal for everything from groups to portraits and children.
● The keen travel photographer might prefer a 24–50mm wide angle zoom.
● The sports enthusiast could benefit from an 80–210mm.
● The portrait photographer is better off with a 70–150mm.
But remember that the real enthusiast will pick a prime lens for his or her best pictures, because they tend to be better optically—so the wide angle man might buy a superb 24mm, and cover with an 80–200mm zoom for all those telephoto lengths he might occasionally need.
● Look for a zoom which balances well in the hand, and which has zoom and focus controls which, whatever the type, are easily distinguished.
● Focus should hold when zooming so that there is no need to re-set it after changing focal length.
● Long zoom lenses, such as 100–300mm, should have a tripod bush for mounting the lens, not the camera.

Advantages

The big advantages of the zoom—fewer lenses to carry, no lens changing, infinitely variable focal lengths—allow the photographer to work quickly and accurately, with less leg work involved in framing the subject properly, and more freedom to select the right viewpoint or moment of subject action.

Disadvantages

The disadvantages of zoom lenses are that they tend to be heavy; they are never as light as a single focal length 'prime' lens, and are often slower in lens speed (smaller maximum aperture)

▶ Cutaway view of telephoto zoom lens. Zoom lenses are made up of groups of lens elements which move to change the focal length and focus. The optics are complex and the number of groups and elements vary from one manufacturer to another. The front elements (below right) twist to focus the lens, the centre section slides or twists to alter the focal length. The rear element is fixed.

▼ The sequence below was taken with a 35–100mm zoom lens from the same point. The first shot, at 35mm (a wide angle covering 62°) takes in the whole scene; 50mm (covering about 47°) is equivalent to a standard lens on a 35mm SLR; 80mm (angle of view about 29°) moves in closer to the climbers; 100mm (angle of view about 24°) has the effect of a medium length telephoto lens.

Focusing   Correcting

Zoom

35mm   50mm   85mm   100mm

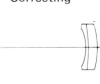

and of lower optical performance.
But if they seem expensive, you only need to add up the prices of two or three single lenses to find that price, at least, is not a disadvantage.

Problems with zooms

Zooms and 'varifocals'—which are zooms which need refocusing after you change the focal length—are prone to a few major faults.

Distortion: straight lines may appear as gentle curves, noticeable with architectural subjects or copying.

Poor coverage: zooms are more likely to have fall-off in sharpness and brightness in the picture corners.

Flare: the multi-element construction of zooms can lead to flare.

Low contrast: the construction can also produce low contrast generally, even in good light.

Curvature of field: zooms may have a curved field, with the centre focusing in a different plane from the edges, especially at close distances.

Picture making

Zoom lenses allow good composition because the photographer does not have to fit subjects into a fixed magnification. They can also make a photographer lazy—he can frame-up with the zoom rather than find a good angle. To get the best shots you need to look for good angles and then use your zoom. Zoom lenses allow you to photograph from a fixed position when you cannot move freely, and also to find the positions which might not be usable with any fixed focal length lens you own.

They also save time spent changing lenses, so that you can catch many shots which you would have missed otherwise. The only exception is if you work with two cameras—for black and white and colour—one zoom between two cameras causes as many hold-ups as two lenses and one camera.

Just as you can pre-set the focus on your normal lens to catch quick shots you can also pre-set the focus control and zoom control on a zoom lens—but not necessarily to the average setting. A 70–210mm zoom is best left at 70mm, because it is much easier to view a wide field and then zoom in than it is to hunt for the subject at 200mm and pull back to frame it. But a 24–50mm zoom could be better left at 50mm.

With a zoom, you can change your viewpoint and angle quickly without losing the precise framing of the

▲ Zoom lenses are ideal for candid shots allowing the photographer to compose a shot quickly.

◄ A 70–150mm zoom lens is useful for portraits. It allows the photographer to work at reasonable distances from the subject.
Roland Michaud

▼ For sports photography, where players move from far to near, an 80–210mm zoom lens is useful. At its longest focal length it is still possible to capture the action, even from a distance.
Don Morley

subject. So moving away 2 metres does not mean getting a smaller image unless you want that to happen. Zooms give you freedom to control perspective as a result of this—notably wide angle zooms. In general photography, where you may not want to devote thought to exact viewpoints, they save time by giving a good frame-filling composition without the necessity of worrying about viewpoint.

Zooms are at their best for photographing people and children. A photographer moving round, closing in and backing off, can be off-putting to adults and children alike. With a zoom you can be less demanding and obtrusive—no more 'back a little more, please', or moving forwards for a closer viewpoint.

Zooms are excellent for sports work, where you can frame-up different points on a track or field from one position without changing lenses. You can use the pre-set focusing techniques for action work, or follow by panning, just as you can with a telephoto, and with push/pull zoom rings, you can often zoom back to catch a moving subject too. Always remember, when following a moving subject with a zoom, that both focus and zoom rings may need changing—the best answer is a zoom with one collar for both.

Zoom lenses are not ideal for landscapes and architecture, mainly because of their characteristics. Though landscape work can be done on zooms, most will give some degree of curvature to straight lines near the edges of the picture—and that includes the horizon. If no horizon is included, then zooms are perfectly acceptable, but in some cases, such as

▼ A zoom is especially useful when your subject is at all nervous. The photographer stays in one place and can change focal length as quickly as if he was focusing.

▶ When covering sporting events the photographer's movement is likely to be limited. Here a zoom comes into its own; no awkward lens changes or weight. *Julian Calder*

calm seascapes with the horizon right against the frame edge, the effect is poor. Architectural shots on wide angle zooms suffer from the same problems, accentuated by the straight lines of architecture.

A familiar effect with a zoom is the long exposure during which the lens is zoomed, producing a rushing or streaked effect. Mount the camera on a tripod, keep the main subject dead centre in the photograph, and use a small f stop so that the exposure is more than 1/8. Press the shutter while operating the zoom control, either increasing or decreasing focal length of the lens. With longer exposures, such as 10 seconds, in low light, a better effect can be had by letting half the exposure be made at a fixed setting and then zooming for the second half.

When you use a zoom, your technique can vary according to the way in which the end result will be produced. If you take colour negatives for sending away to be developed and printed, always make a point of composing the shot exactly, but allow a little margin on the length of the photograph as most prints are not as long and narrow as the 35mm shape. For slides, you can use the full area that you see on the screen, and zooms help you to do this perfectly.

If you print your own photographs from negatives, you can plan for odd shapes—square prints, or long thin prints—by imagining the result on the camera screen. But using a zoom still helps you get the sharpest and least grainy prints by making full use of the negative. And if you zoom carefully, composing accurately, you will not need to change enlargement during a session. So you can keep to standard exposure and filtration settings for all the shots on your roll of film.

Practical aspects

Exposure metering: there is no need for special methods when metering zoom lenses—they behave just like prime lenses of their focal length. But you can use the zoom facility to take selective meter readings or cut out bright sky areas before setting the correct focal length.

Focusing screens: because zooms are sometimes of low aperture—the f5 100–300mm for example—focusing screen aids, such as split image wedges, may not work. For long telephoto zooms a plain ground-glass screen is the best solution. Otherwise, expect zooms to be a little harder to focus generally than other lenses. A bright screen is best.

Aperture changes: many zooms have a variable maximum aperture—that is, 35–100mm, f3·5 to f4·3, meaning that at 35mm the lens has a maximum aperture of f3·5, but at 100mm this drops to f4·3, a half stop change. Always check whether the rest of the scale—f5·6, f8, f11, f16, f22—is linked to this change or not. In some types of zoom, setting f8 at 100mm would actually give you f9·5 because there is no compensation. In others, it would give you f8 correctly. Open aperture

▲ A zoom lens made it possible to shoot this picture cutting out the photographer's shadow. *John Garret*

◄ Expressing movement with a zoom; alter focal length during a long exposure to give double blur. *Gerry Cranham*

▶ Panning and altering the zoom setting gives another impression of speed. *John McGovren*

▼ A wide angle zoom at shortest focal length. *David Kilpatrick.*

metering systems automatically compensate—but flashguns, for example, do not.

Changes in depth of field: remember that you should always pre-view your depth of field at working aperture and working focal length. It changes if you zoom, and checking it at 80mm does not help you judge the result at 135mm.

Changes in focus setting: although zooms are meant to hold accurate focus when you zoom, many do not. There is a slight variation, within acceptable limits. However, if you focus quickly at 70mm and then zoom, without checking, to shoot at 210mm, there may be enough error to give you a bad picture. So always either focus at the longest focal length, or at the setting you use to take the picture.

Lens hood, flare and filters: always use a hood if possible, and avoid shooting into the light without first checking the stopped-down effect, as flare patches may appear with many zooms. Check that hoods and filters do not cause cut-off at short focal lengths by

taking a picture set at infinity and fully stopped down.

Filter threads: most zooms now have moderately normal filter fittings—tele-zooms may have threads as small as 49mm but are more usually around the 55–62mm mark. In camera makers' series of lenses, the zooms often have the standard thread. Mid-range zooms and wide angle zooms, however, are far more likely to have very large filter threads—62mm, 67mm or even 72mm. Filters in these sizes sometimes have very thick rims which can cut off corners, so check before buying.

Mounts: most zooms today come from independent makers, and nearly all of them are available in the popular camera fittings and with interchangeable mounts. Because zooms from independent makers are often just as good as camera makers' lenses (if available) and normally a fraction of the price, buying an intermount lens is a very good policy. Even if you change your other lenses when you change your camera, you can keep the zoom.

Using a single flash

If you own a camera the chances are that you will also own a flash gun. There are many situations where the light is low, and you can't take the pictures you want without one. A single flash gun is more versatile than you may think. All the pictures in this article were taken using just one gun.

An electronic flash gun allows you to take well exposed and very sharp pictures under a wide variety of conditions. The flash itself lasts a very short time (1/1,000-1/50,000 second). This brief duration 'freezes' subject movement and prevents camera shake. The light quality is similar to daylight, so no special films or filters are needed.

Most flash guns have built-in photo cell sensors to give automatic exposure. Power is usually supplied by ordinary batteries. One set will provide a large number of flashes. Some flash units use rechargeable accumulators or mains current as well.

Check your camera instructions for correct synchronization settings. Most 35mm SLRs must be set to 1/60 or 1/125.

Using flash

Use a flash gun when the existing light is too dim to allow a suitable hand held exposure. Remember that a flash gun, particularly 'on-camera', gives its own very distinctive light quality. Some flash pictures can be disappointing because the appeal of the subject depended partly on natural light quality. Indirect bounce flash can give more natural results.

Fluorescent or electric lighting can be bright enough to allow hand held shots without flash. Slides shot in this way show a strong colour cast. Using a flash gun ensures that the colours appear normally.

At a party a flash gun gives accurate exposures, captures the action and prevents camera shake—no matter how good the party! An automatic gun is best. For indoor sports a flash gun is almost essential to freeze the rapid movements of the athletes.

Equipment choice

A small manual gun costs little more than a roll of slide film. You have to use a table of guide numbers (GN) to calculate the correct exposure. Larger 'computer' units have more features but are more expensive. They are much easier and quicker to use, since the built-in sensor gives automatic exposure control. Automatic *thyristor* control also saves battery power and can cut recycling times considerably.

Some SLRs are designed to take special automatic flash guns which use the camera's own TTL metering system for exposure control. These are known as TTL OTF flash guns.

Direct flash—on-camera

On-camera flash is most convenient. It gives predictable, flat lighting with harsh, dark shadows. Light intensity falls off rapidly as distance increases, so backgrounds are under-exposed. This dark effect can be used to suppress a messy background. When a subject has depth, it is difficult to give correct exposure to each part. In a smoky atmosphere light reflects strongly from smoke closest to the camera. Pictures come out flat and with weak colours.

Since the flash gun is close to the camera, light can reflect straight back into the lens. This causes the 'red-eye' effect. Spectacles, windows, mirrors and gloss paint can all cause ugly bright spots and patches in the same way. Avoid having such surfaces facing straight towards the camera.

The best pictures taken with on-camera flash have: unimportant backgrounds; subjects at roughly equal distances from the camera; and reflective surfaces angled away from the lens.

Direct flash—off-camera

Some problems with on-camera flash can be solved by using an extension lead. With a portrait it is usually better to have the light coming from above and to one side. Shadows on the face give roundness and add interest.

When a subject has considerable depth the flash gun can be placed to one side at roughly the same distance from each important part. Exposure is then the same for all areas. Shadows are still harsh, but can be made to fall out of sight by holding the flash gun well above the camera.

Used from below, a flash gun gives a sinister quality to most subjects—try it! With the flash gun to one side, reflections bounce away from the lens. Red eye is avoided by moving the gun just a few centimetres from the camera. Many modern cameras do not have a separate flash sync socket. You need a hot-shoe to 3mm sync socket adapter, before an extension lead can be used with these.

Bounce flash

Some guns have tilting heads, so you can use them on-camera to give *indirect* lighting. Point your flash gun at a ceiling or wall instead of the subject. The large patch of illumination on the ceiling effectively becomes the light source. Shadows are softer and the lighting is even over a reasonable distance.

The reflective surface must be white or grey if you want accurate colours. If there isn't a convenient ceiling or wall, a sheet of white card can be used. Special 'bounce brackets' are made for some bounce-head guns. These hold a small sheet of card to act as an artificial ceiling. For a greater variety of effects you can use a white, silver or gold flash umbrella. Fitting your flash gun and reflector to a stand leaves you free to hand-hold the camera.

Bounce light from a ceiling can be most natural looking. With a portrait, angle the gun to bounce the light midway between camera and sitter. This will give soft shadows on the face with adequate lighting in the eyes and background. If the light bounces directly over the sitter, shadows under the eyes and nose will be too dark. With the flash bounced off a wall or card the effect of window light can be created. The soft shadow quality is perfect for revealing textures and shapes. Reflections in shiny objects are full of interest.

Much of the output is lost when flash is bounced. Light is absorbed and reflected uselessly away. The sensor can still be used, for auto exposure control, but it must face the subject. Some guns have a detachable or accessory sensor which can be used on a remote lead.

Set on 'auto', a flash gun could fire at maximum output and still under-expose the subject. To avoid this problem, some flash guns have a 'check light'. You fire the gun by pressing the 'open flash' button, while looking at the control panel. If there is sufficient light for correct exposure the sensor will switch on an LED.

Film and filters

Colour film should be daylight balance. Any black and white emulsion can be used. Film speed is an important consideration, especially for bounce flash. Light wastage is high so fast film becomes essential. At parties you may use both direct and bounce flash, so a high speed film (400 ASA) and an automatic flashgun make the best combination.

For colour slide photography, direct flash is sometimes a little blue. A pale yellow (CC05Y) or skylight (8IA) filter removes this cast. Filters can either be fitted over the camera lens or the flash gun.

Direct flash—on-camera

▲ One flash gun mounted on the camera gives little texture or detail, harsh shadows and an unflattering effect. The model here was close to the background (approx 2ft or 2/3 metre), creating a noticeable shadow. To avoid this, position your subject further from the background (approx 9ft or 3 metres).

Direct flash—off-camera

▲ Using one flash gun fixed to a bracket or held slightly to the side and above the camera gives a better result than with the gun on the camera. The result is softer and more flattering. In this shot there is no background shadow as the model had been moved away from the background.

Indirect flash—on-camera

▲ An on-camera flash with a tilting head can be bounced off a ceiling or wall (must be light coloured) for a soft effect. Bouncing reduces the light reaching the subject, so with manual flash units, you must increase the amount of exposure—as a guide, open the aperture by two stops.

Indirect flash—off-camera

▲ The best possible picture that can be taken with one flash gun is when the flash is held away from the camera and a reflector (eg a piece of white card) is placed at the side of the subject to act as a fill in. This produces a natural looking picture. All photographs by *John Evans*.

COMMON FAULTS

1. *Light fall off* occurs as distance increases. With the limited coverage of one gun don't expect to be able to record large areas of detail.
2. Large subjects can have an *uneven depth of exposure.* For correct exposure place the flash gun equidistant from the important parts of the subject.
3. To avoid the *'red eye'* effect move your flash gun so that it is slightly away from the line of the lens.
4. Shiny reflective surfaces cause *unwanted bright spots* in a photograph. Do not have shiny surfaces pointing directly at the camera.
5. *Smoke* in the atmosphere indoors makes pictures look dull. Look at the atmosphere before shooting.

Key words for understanding flash

Automatic exposure: a photocell sensor measures the light reflectd from the subject. When sufficient is received the sensor shuts off the flash tube. In use, choose an aperture according to the film speed. Set this on the camera lens. Set the film speed on the gun and you are ready to shoot. (A choice of apertures is sometimes possible.)
With a light background or clothing you will get under exposure. A dark background will give over exposure. Compensate by opening or closing lens aperture.

Dedicated flash: special flash gun which sets camera's shutter and in some cases may also have TTL exposure metering.
Flash duration: the length of time for which the flash fires. With an auto gun this is controlled by the sensor and varies between 1/1,000 and 1/50,000th second. With a manual gun it is fixed at between 1/1,000 and 1/5,000.

Fluorescent light: strip-tube lighting. It usually gives strong green cast with slide film.
Guide Number (GN): indication of power output. Also a means of calculating correct exposure with a manual flash gun. Correct aperture = GN divided by flash gun to subject distance.
Manual exposure: cheaper guns don't have auto control. The flash fires on full power and exposure is read off a table on the gun. Look up film speed, then subject distance: read off correct aperture for those conditions.
Open flash: a button on the flash gun, sometimes marked 'test'. Press this to fire the flash for special effects or in the 'check light' procedure.

Recycling time: time needed for flash gun to recharge after firing Recharge is shown by a 'ready light' glowing on the control panel. (Time can be very short with an auto gun used close to the subject.)
Synchronization: making sure the flash fires at the time that the shutter is open. This is most important with SLRs, since focal plane shutters cause partial exposure only if the wrong speed is set. Most guns can be used up to 1/60, some up to 1/125. Check with the camera instruction book, if in doubt.
Thyristor circuit: electronic component in an auto-exposure gun which saves any charge not used in one flash and enables it to be used for the next flash shot.

These mushrooms were shot with only one flash, placed slightly to the left and above the camera. *Heather Angel*

Using two or more flashes

Using more than one flash gun opens up a new world of exciting portraits and special effects. Natural or studio style lighting effects can be created. You can lighten backgrounds, and show the colours of your subjects more clearly. Large areas can be successfully lit with a little forethought and care, using a number of flash guns synchronized together. (In certain circumstances it is possible to use one gun flashed a number of times.)

Film choice

Any film can be used, but as with all flash photography, colour film must be daylight balanced.

In many cases exposures will be good approximations at best. Slide film has little tolerance to incorrect exposure. Negative film (colour and black and white) has better latitude, particularly to over-exposure. This material is thus the best choice for complex multi-exposure shots. Aim to slightly over-expose the film. If your calculations are wrong, you'll usually get an acceptable result! Record your exposure data so that successful shots can be repeated and mistakes avoided in the future.

Flash gun power

When using several flash guns together no special guns are needed. However, it could save you money to buy guns of different sizes.

Most lighting sets need a main light. Its job is to provide the quality and basic lighting direction. A 'main light' flash gun is normally the most powerful. Other flash guns are used as background or 'fill-in' lights. These can be less powerful. A typical home studio portrait might need three flash guns, one large and two smaller ones.

Synchronized flash

Synchronizing several guns to fire together is the most convenient way of working. Two ways of doing this are using slave units or a multiple adaptor. **A slave unit** is a photo cell which 'sees' only flash light. It is fitted to a flash gun placed some distance from the camera. The main light flash is connected as usual to the camera via the hot shoe or 3mm socket. When the main flash fires, the slave triggers the remote gun. (There is no significant delay between flashes.) Flash guns may be placed anywhere providing the slave units clearly 'see' one other gun which is firing. Any number of guns can be synchronized in this way. The flash guns can be different models.

▲ To obtain the soft natural effect in this shot, two flash guns were used. The main gun was to the left, and slightly higher than the camera. Fill-in flash on the camera softened the shadows from the main gun. *J Pfaff.*

▶ Three guns were used for this shot. One covered with a green gel lit the background. A large brolly flash at the right-hand side lit the hair and shoulders. A small brolly flash lit the model from the front. *Sanders*

Key words for understanding flash

Synchronization: making sure the flash fires the same time that the shutter fully opens. With multi-flash, it also involves making sure that all the flash guns fire at the same time.

Bounce lighting: reflecting flashlight from a card, ceiling or wall, so light quality is soft and even. Surfaces should be light or white to avoid false colours. On auto, the sensor must face the subject.

Lighting ratio: the relationship between the brightest part of a subject and the darkest. With a colour portrait a ratio of 3:1 is best.

Check light or confidence light: device on a larger flash gun which shows when enough light is reflected from the subject to give proper exposure.

Crossed shadows: two or more shadows pointing in opposite directions. Caused by using flash guns of similar power on either side of the camera. Particularly undesirable in a portrait, where having a shadow on both sides of the nose is unpleasant. The remedy is to bring one gun closer to the camera.

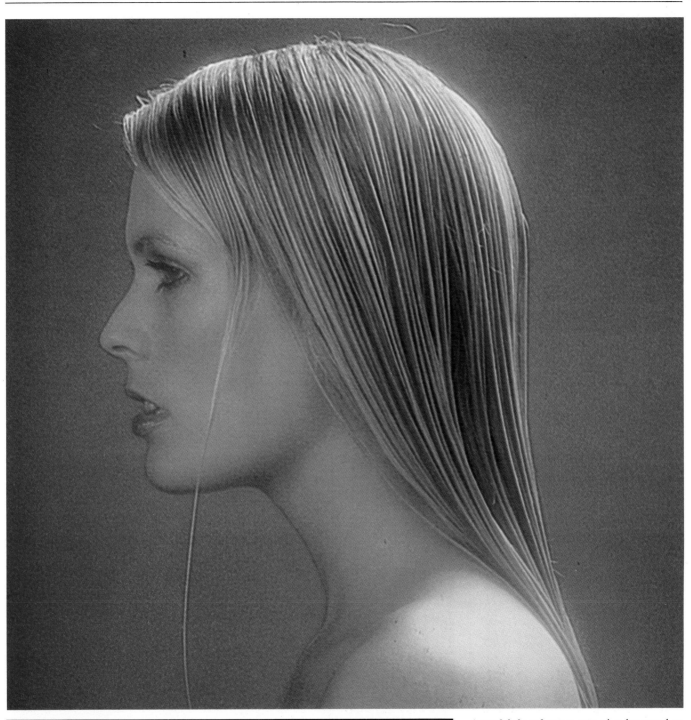

Controlling the exposure for fill-in flash

Exposure may be controlled fully automatically if each flash lights a separate area. When flashes overlap, as with main and fill-in guns use the following method to get a 3:1 (main to fill-in) lighting ratio:
1) set main light gun on auto
2) set actual film speed on main gun
3) select suitable aperture
4) set the fill-in gun on manual
5) assume film speed for fill-in gun is 3x actual (*eg* set 400 ASA on the flash for 125 ASA film)
6) position fill-in gun at distance to give 'correct' exposure with 'false' film speed, at selected aperture.
Result: fill-in alone will be one third as bright as main light plus fill-in.

A multiple adaptor can also be used to link up to three flash guns. In this case, the guns must be the same.
The adaptor has three camera-type 3mm sockets and a single 3mm 'plug'. Each gun is connected to a socket via an extension lead. A fourth lead links the adaptor to the camera. Location of the flash guns is limited by the lengths of the leads. Beware of including a lead in the shot!
Many SLR's have both a hot shoe and

a 3mm sync socket. It is sometimes possible to connect one flash gun to each. This produces the simplest method of synchronizing two guns. Check your camera or contact the camera's distributor to see if you can use your camera in this way, or you may cause damage.

Multi-exposure flash

This technique can only be used in a darkened room or outside at night. Put your camera on a tripod and set the shutter to 'B'. Keep the shutter open with a locking cable release. One flash gun can then be fired several times to build up complex lighting effects. Don't touch the camera between flashes: any movement will give you an unwanted multiple image. Remember to close the shutter after the last flash.

Subject approach

Many subjects benefit from multi-flash lighting. A portrait lit with *one gun* has harsh heavy shadows and a dark background. Use a *second gun* to lighten the shadows on the face. This fill-in flash should have about 1/3 the power of the main flash.

The fill-in gun should not create its own strong shadows, so it needs to be quite close to the camera. Keep it about 30cm

from the camera lens or you could get 'red eye.'

You can soften the fill-in light by taping white tissue over the gun or bouncing it from a reflector. A third gun, placed behind the sitter, lightens the background and burns out ugly shadows. The power needed for this gun varies according to the distances involved and the effect wanted. The third gun could, alternatively, be used as a hair or rim light. Placed behind the sitter it is pointed back towards the hair or shoulders. The resulting halo of light clearly separates sitter from background.

Figure studies, groups and formal portraits can all be photographed in a similar way. Synchronized flash is essential.

Multi-exposures: other uses

Night-time exteriors or interiors can be shot by multi exposing or 'painting' with a series of flashes. You can even walk right into the picture area. To fire the gun use the *open flash* button, often marked 'test'.

Both you and the flash gun should be hidden from view behind furniture or in doorways. Exposure can be on auto. Each flash should light one area. Overlapping flashes cause patches of over-

exposure. Try to keep the flash guns pointing roughly in the same directions: crossed shadows look ugly.

One gun multi-exposures

You can also multi-expose on a smaller scale at home, though subject choice is limited to still life and other static objects.

Lighting can be built up to resemble synchronized multi-flash, with one gun doing the work of three.

For example, have one flash from the side of the camera to give a main light, bounce it from a reflector for fill-in, and then from the ceiling for a top light. The combinations are endless. Bizarre effects and ghostly multi-images are produced by moving parts of the subject between flashes.

Exposure calculation can be awkward when two flashes light the same area. When using an auto gun, you must alter the film speed setting for each flash to persuade the gun to emit different amounts of light. For a 3:1 (main: fill-in) lighting ratio, set the gun as follows:
1) main flash—increase film speed by $1\frac{1}{2}\times$ (*eg* set 200 for 125 ASA film).
2) fill in flash—increase film speed by $3\times$ (*eg* set 400 ASA for 125 ASA film). This will give the correct final result.

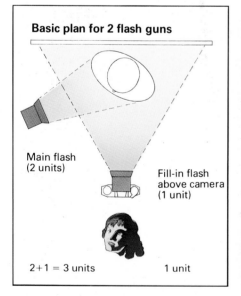

Basic plan for 2 flash guns

Main flash (2 units)

Fill-in flash above camera (1 unit)

2+1 = 3 units   1 unit

▲ ▶ Two flashes were used in this shot, illuminating the highlights together. The fill-in lights the shadows (caused by the main flash) alone. It is rare in a portrait for the fill-in light NOT to illuminate the highlights as well as the shadows. Main gun gives 2 units light. Fill-in gives 1 unit light. Total on highlight side is 3(2+1). Total on shadow side is 1. Ratio is 3:1.

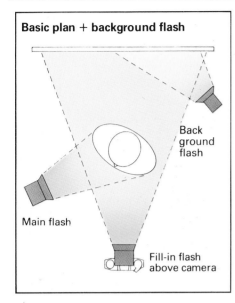

Basic plan + background flash

Back ground flash

Main flash

Fill-in flash above camera

▲ ▶ A third gun can be added to the basic two flash portrait set up. In this shot a third gun was placed behind the model and directed at the background. This flash lightens the background and separates it from the subject giving it more depth. This third gun must be positioned carefully. You must make sure that the gun will not be visible in the photograph.

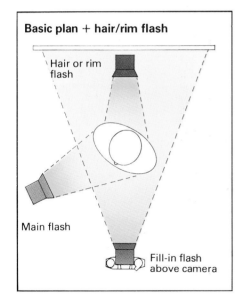

Basic plan + hair/rim flash

Hair or rim flash

Main flash

Fill-in flash above camera

▲ ▶ An alternative way to use the third flash gun is as a hair or rim light. The gun should be in the same position as for the background flash only it should point back towards the hair or shoulders. It creates a ring of light around these areas. The brightness of the effect depends on the power of the gun and the distance it is from the subject. All pictures *J Evans*

Tripods and supports

Have you ever taken a series of photographs and then found that the prints or slides have all come out looking inexplicably blurred? A special occasion, impossible to repeat, becomes a hazy memory; a rare scenic view comes out looking fuzzy. Both results are not worth a slide mount or the space in the family album.

You have spent time and effort getting a good photograph, the exposure is correct and the focus is perfect, yet the end result is a disappointment. The cause is probably camera shake. This happens if the photographer moves the camera during the actual moment of exposure. Only very slight movement is enough to spoil a picture—and it is easily done, even by the most experienced photographer. But it is a problem that is easily put right by supporting the camera properly.

Resting the camera

If you hold the camera by hand for most shots it is important to know how to support it firmly. Think of yourself as a human tripod when holding the camera; stand firmly with legs slightly apart, and hold the camera rigidly in both hands with elbows tucked into your sides. This position should allow you to balance the camera firmly, but allow some movement so that you can compose the picture. When you take the picture, squeeze the shutter release slowly to avoid shaking the camera. Or bend down on one knee and rest your elbow on the other knee. In this position it is easier to hold the camera vertically. The camera can also be held reasonably steady by putting the camera strap around your neck and taking up the slack by winding the strap around one hand. Another way of steadying the camera is to attach a length of chain (available as an accessory) to it. The end of the chain is held under the foot so that the camera is under tension. This method has limited application as it can't be used in all positions and the camera can still be moved sideways.

Of course you do not always have to hand hold the camera. You may sometimes be able to place the camera on a

▲ The chances of camera shake are more likely with slow shutter speeds or when using a long lens. Use any available support to lean against in order to hold the camera steady.

◄ A combination of fast shutter speed, adequate camera support and sharp focusing produced this shot of a cyclist.

▼ This series shows: the effect of camera shake—an overall appearance of movement in one direction; too slow a shutter speed; camera held steady but wrongly focused.

wall, or hold it against a tree or lamp-post, to give it extra support. If the camera is balanced on a wall, make sure the surface is as even as possible and that there are no awkward bumps. If you are using supports you can minimize camera movement still further by using a cable release, if the camera takes one. The shutter can then be triggered through the release without the photographer touching the camera.

Cable releases

It is usually a good idea to use a cable release and some other form of support at speeds of less than 1/60.

Cable releases are available in various lengths and can be as long as 3 metres. The most common cable release is about 20cm and this is suitable for most purposes. Longer releases are pneumatically operated. Electronically operated cameras may need a special type of cable release.

Always take your camera with you when buying accessories to make sure they are suitable for your particular make and type of camera.

Reciprocity failure

With the camera on a tripod and using a cable release it is feasible to photograph in bad light with a slow shutter speed. In reality it is not so simple.

Under normal lighting conditions various combinations of shutter speed and aperture can be used to expose film correctly. However, in extreme lighting conditions film does not behave as it should.

For example, if the light is very low and the meter reading indicates a long exposure, the film may be underexposed despite using settings which are apparently correct. This is known as reciprocity law failure, and is caused by the emulsion being less sensitive to dim light over a long exposure than it is to short bursts of bright light. Exposures longer than 1/8 with colour film and 1 second with black and white will need additional exposure, but all films vary and the manufacturer's instructions usually give details. With colour there may be a colour shift as well, needing a corrective filter. This also applies with very short exposures—speeds

faster than 1/1000 and some types of flash. At both exposure extremes think of the film as being slower than its given ASA.

Tripods and monopods

These are custom-made supports which find their way into many photographers' gadget bags.

A monopod is a one-legged camera support, with height adjustment, and usually a spike at one end so that it can be driven into soft ground for firm support. The monopod is portable and easy to use, although most have no head adjustment for altering the angle of the camera and do not give the same firmness as a tripod.

Tripods are available in various sizes, from small lightweight models which are ideal for carrying in the gadget bag, to the heavyweight studio types. Table-top tripods are light and easy to assemble. They are most useful for indoor photography, where they can be set up on a table or chair. Because these tripods are so light they should only be used with light cameras—they are not sturdy enough for heavy models.

Small and medium-sized tripods come in a wide range and offer the photographer the most choice. Most are reasonably priced, are made of aluminium and have quick-release extending legs which means they can be set up quickly and easily. Many models have

**1–5 Cable releases are available in various lengths.
6 Pneumatic release allows longer distances than cable releases.
7 Electronic shutter release allows the photographer to operate an auto winder from a distance.**

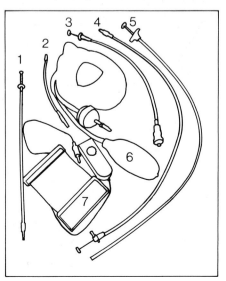

a pan and tilt head. This is an adjustable top which can be tilted back and forth and panned from side to side. The more expensive models have extra struts on the centre column of the tripod for extra rigidity. Some centre columns also have gears and a rotating handle so that the camera can be moved up and down quickly.

Some tripods also have a built-in cable release (or provision for one) so that you can trigger the shutter without touching the camera or tripod, thus lessening the risk of camera shake even more. Some tripods can also be folded almost flat on the ground for low-angle shots.

Heavy-duty tripods are designed for professionals and the advanced amateur. Because of their size, they are extremely sturdy and are ideal for supporting large cameras, or cameras with long and perhaps heavy lenses. Obviously, they are not as portable as the smaller models and are therefore mainly used in studios. Heavy-duty tripods are usually quite expensive, but offer great rigidity and firmness and a large degree of adjustment.

Using a tripod

A tripod is a very versatile camera support and with so many models available in the medium price bracket, it is the kind of accessory that every photographer should consider buying.

Despite the increasing use of highspeed film, many photographers still prefer to use slower emulsions for some of their work. With these slower films a tripod is essential in low-light situations where a long exposure is needed. At night, for example, an exposure time of a few seconds may be necessary even with fast film. Some form of support is essential when using a telephoto lens. The longer the lens, the more important the support becomes, and in some instances the lens itself is supported rather than the camera. For fast action photography, where you may need to follow a moving object precisely, a tripod with a pan head is very useful. The camera can be moved with the subject, with the photographer taking shots at random. Indoor photography is another area where the tripod is most useful, particularly when using flash. If the camera is supported on the tripod and the photographer uses a cable release, he can move away, perhaps to distract the sitter or to hold a flash for more interesting lighting. However the tripod is used, it is not just another accessory—it can be a vital part of the photographer's equipment.

● To make a medium-sized tripod more secure a weighted bag can be suspended from the central column of the tripod.

▼ **Left: a weighted bag, suspended from the central column of a lightweight tripod makes the tripod more steady as it lowers the centre of gravity. This is particularly useful in windy weather and when using a long telephoto lens.**

▼ **There are various types of table-top tripod (from left): Compact tripod which doubles as a shoulder stock. A sturdy model with pan and tilt head for any camera position. A small lightweight tripod for indoor use.**

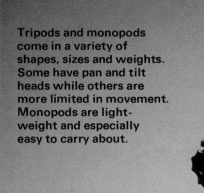

Tripods and monopods
come in a variety of
shapes, sizes and weights.
Some have pan and tilt
heads while others are
more limited in movement.
Monopods are light-
weight and especially
easy to carry about.

Close-up lenses

Close-up photography can reveal a whole new world of interest and excitement—the extraordinary or beautiful details we normally miss in insects and flowers, or abstract images and patterns to be found in nature. To capture on film the detail you can see quite easily with your eyes, the camera needs some facility to be able to focus close-up on a small object. Close-up lenses, depending on their magnification, also reveal what the eyes miss.

There is a whole range of equipment for doing this, but basically they all provide a way of taking the camera closer in to the subject than the normal closest focusing setting, usually about 45cm for the standard lens of an SLR. This makes it possible to photograph small objects from close-up, sometimes at their actual size and sometimes magnifying them, depending on the equipment being used.

This article deals with close-up lenses which are attached to the front of the camera's lens. Separate articles deal with extension tubes and reversing rings, macro lenses and bellows, all of which are used for close-up photography. The first two—close-up attachments and extension tubes—are the cheapest but before deciding on any particular system, consider all the possibilities.

The 35mm SLR camera has totally changed the ability of amateur photographers to take impressive close-up studies of a variety of subjects without technical difficulties. Until quite recently, photographers used to work with complex tables, viewing attachments and measuring devices in order to photograph something as simple as a rose. The SLR camera gives a precise view of the subject, however close the photographer chooses to go, right up to producing it life-size on the film, a magnification ratio of 1:1. The subject appears greatly magnified on a projection screen and even three or four times larger than life in an ordinary print.

Close-up lens attachments

By far the easiest equipment to use is the close-up attachment which screws on the front rim of the lens, and works rather like a magnifying glass. It focuses the lens at a closer distance than normal. Distances from one meter down to 10cm away are possible using a close-up attachment on a standard 50mm lens.

The advantage of these attachments is that no change in exposure is required,

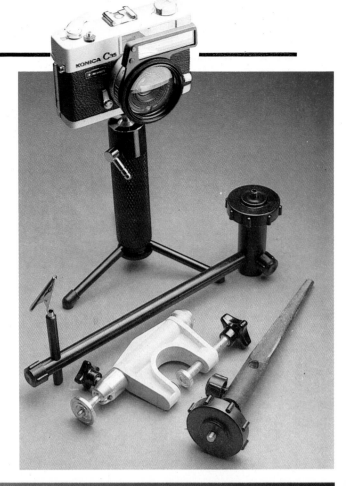

▶ 1 A rangefinder camera fitted with a close-up attachment is supported on a table-top tripod.
2 One end of the support attachment screws into the camera like a tripod and is adjustable. The clip at the other end is used to grip the item being photographed.
3 A G-clamp is a useful support for close-up work where a tripod would be too cumbersome.
4 A ground spike allows low angle shots.

▼ Close-up attachments are available in various strengths and with different thread sizes so they can be used on most 35mm SLR cameras. The attachments do not affect the light entering the lens so they are easy to use on cameras without TTL metering systems.

making them easy to use with cameras without through-the-lens metering. They can also be fitted to a lens of almost any focal length, whether standard or telephoto, although wide angle lenses are not particularly successful, and they will always focus on their dioptric focal length whether on a 50mm or 135mm lens. (1 diopter focuses at 1000mm, 2 at 500mm, 3 at 333mm, and so on.) Obviously this makes for really good close-ups with telephoto lenses. The disadvantage of close-up attachments is that, because they are optical, they can cause a loss of sharpness by conflicting with the

◀ A close-up attachment which incorporates extending legs supports a rangefinder camera for close-up work.

▼ Dandelions have an appealing symmetrical pattern that is enhanced by close-up shots. With a standard lens at its shortest focusing distance a group of dandelions (far left) is visible. As the strength of the close-up attachments increase so the focusing distance is decreased making it possible to move right in on an individual dandelion (below left) and a close-up of it (below).

50mm lens	plus 0·7 diopter	plus 1·5 diopters

▲ Lupins photographed with a standard 50mm lens on an SLR, 1/15 second at f8 on Kodachrome. Close-up attachments were added to decrease the focusing distance for this series of close-ups.

▼ Two shots with a 4·5 diopter attachment: f8 (left) gives sufficient depth of field for an overall sharp image; f2 narrows the depth of field so that the sides of the flower farthest from the camera are out of focus.

highly corrected design of the prime lens, but normally this is hardly noticeable, especially when a small aperture such as f8, f11 or f16 is being used.

Basic close-up lenses are made in various strengths, which refer to their diopters; 1, 2 and 3 diopters are the more common ones and can be bought individually. The larger the number, the closer the lens can focus. The lenses can be used in conjunction with each other; for example, the 1, 2 and 3

diopter lenses can be used together to function as 6 diopters. Make sure the strongest diopter is next to the prime lens if using 2 or more close-up lenses.

Variable close-up lenses use more than one optical element and are much more powerful, often up to 10 or more diopters, focusing the lens as close as 10cm, which produces an image about half life-size on the film. They are more expensive than ordinary close-up lenses and often give less good results but they are convenient.

Achromatic lenses are similar to 1, 2 and 3 diopter close-up lenses but usually consist of more than one element. They are designed to avoid colour aberrations and colour fringing, which breaks down the light to give a rainbow effect, producing sharper than normal results and costing several times as much as simple single-glass close-up lenses.

Practical aspects

Viewing and focusing is very critical with close-ups. The best focusing screen for close-ups is a plain ground-glass one. With SLR screens which are not interchangeable, use the ground-glass part of the screen for best results.

▶ *Eric Crichton* photographs this series. To get even lighting he uses white card to reflect light on to the subject. A flash can be bounced off the card or used to fill in. Use a tripod so that the shutter speed can allow an aperture of f8 or smaller.

4·5 diopters at f8	4·5 diopters at f2

plus 3 diopters

plus 4·5 diopters

plus15 diopters

Choosing film

Using the correct film can make all the difference between a disappointing picture and a highly successful one. So it is important to know the full range of films available for your camera—or the one you may be thinking of buying next. It is a question of matching the film to the type of photography you are doing. Some films are better for poor light conditions or fast-moving subjects, others can reproduce the tiniest detail of a flower. Some colour films produce colour prints, others produce slides for the projector; there are films for daylight and indoor electric (tungsten) light. Some you can process yourself, others must be factory-processed.

When buying a film you need to decide on:
● **Type** do you want colour prints, colour slides or black and white prints?
● **Size:** is the film available in the correct size for your camera?
● **Exposures:** how many are needed?
● **Speed:** is it the right film for the particular lighting conditions?

The most common sizes available today are 110, disc, 35mm cassettes, and 120 roll film. 110/disc is fairly limited in types and speeds available, while the other two come in a much wider range. So if you plan to buy a new camera, bear this in mind. This article deals with the more standard types of film. Film for instant-print cameras, view cameras and other specialist films are covered later.

Packaging
Film is always sold packed in light-proof wrapping in a box marked with its *size, type, speed* and *number of exposures*. It is available in three main forms—cartridges, cassettes and roll film.

Cartridges: 110 and 126 (Instamatic) films are packed in plastic drop-in cartridges. These are the easiest films to load, but are only used with the less expensive eye-level viewfinder cameras. The drawbacks with them are that each exposure costs more than on other types and the cartridge cannot hold the film firmly enough against the back of the camera to produce really sharp pictures. Disc film is more compact but can only be used for colour prints.

35mm cassettes hold double perforated film. They are used in some eye-level viewfinders, rangefinders and in most SLR cameras.

Roll film is used in TLRs and large-format SLRs, and some older models of viewfinder cameras. It is protected by a backing paper which is longer than the film and so protects it from light at the beginning and end.

Film and backing are supplied wound tightly on to a spool with a wide flange to protect the edges of the film.

Picture format
The camera you use determines the format and size of the negative. The format will either be square or rectangular. The square formats are 126, 127 and 120 (6 x 6cm) roll film, and all the rest are rectangular.

Size
The actual size of the negative affects the quality of any enlargements: the larger the size of each negative, the better the quality of the enlargement. Even so, the quality of most modern films is such that large prints can be made from small negatives. Even a 110 cartridge negative, taken on a camera with a good quality lens, can be enlarged up to 20 x 15cm without loss of detail. Poster size prints can be made from 120 roll film with similar detail.

Cartridges
● *110 film:* the small negative is difficult to view without enlargement; contact prints are of very limited value. 12 or 20 exposures.
● *126 film:* uses film 35mm wide with single perforations. Used in some eye-level viewfinder cameras. 12 or 20 exposures.

35mm cassettes
● *135 film:* this size gives the widest variety of film types. 20, 24 or 36 exposures. It is also available in bulk lengths for loading into cassettes in the darkroom.

A few cameras take half frame negatives, using the same cassettes but giving double the number of exposures.

Roll film
● *127 film:* used in older eye-level viewfinder cameras. 12 exposures.
● *120 film:* according to the camera, this film allows negative sizes 6 x 6cm (known in the past as 2¼ square). 12 exposures. Also comes in 6 x 7cm (10 exposures), 6 x 4·5cm (15 or 16 exposures), and 6 x 9cm (8 exposures). Used in TLRs, roll-film SLRs (like the Hasselblad), and some older types of viewfinder cameras.

● *120 double perforated film:* negative size 6 x 6cm. Used in roll-film SLRs. Only available in bulk lengths for loading into special magazines.
● *220 film:* exactly the same negative

sizes (6 x 6cm) as for 120 film, but the film is twice as long, giving 24 exposures, and has no paper backing.

Take care

● **Film date** When you buy a film check the date stamp on the package. Out-of-date film may be all right, but you have no recompense if the film is faulty.

● **Avoid heat** Don't leave film where it will get too hot, such as the back window or dashboard of a car. Films tend to deteriorate in humid conditions, or when subjected to chemical fumes.

● **Light protection** Put each exposed roll of film back in its lightproof wrapping or tin until it is processed. Remember, exposed film deteriorates more quickly than unexposed, so have it processed promptly.

● **Loading/unloading film** Never load or unload film (particularly fast film of 400 ASA or more) in bright light, but only indoors or in deep shadows.

● **Dust and dirt** Before you load a new film always check that there is no dust or dirt inside the camera. These can scratch the film.

● **Jammed film** If you feel sudden resistance when winding on the film do not force it; take the camera into a darkroom. Open the camera back and reposition the cassette. You may have to improvise a darkroom by using a coat or jacket, a cupboard, or even by crawling under the bedclothes.

● **On holiday** It is best to buy film before you go. Often more expensive abroad, and you are sure of having up-to-date, well-stored film of the type you want.

● **Used film** Always bend the end of exposed film over (or wind it right into the cassette) so that you don't re-load it as a new film.

● **Packing film** When travelling, make sure that films are not packed into baggage that will be x-rayed—this applies to exposed and unexposed film equally. Keep it in your hand baggage and ask the security officer to check it by hand.

● **Processing** Have films processed as soon as possible after finishing the roll, as exposed film deteriorates more quickly than unexposed film, particularly if left in hot conditions.

● **Loading** Make sure that the film loads smoothly on to the take up spool, that none of the perforations are bent or torn, and that both sets of perforations mesh smoothly with the sprockets before closing the camera back.

FILM FORMATS
The range of picture sizes shown actual size. (They are generally described by the dimensions printed alongside, although in practice some cameras give slightly smaller pictures as shown.)

110 cartridge (13 x 17mm)

126 cartridge (28 x 28mm)

35mm cassette (36 x 24mm)

35mm cassette half frame (18 x 24mm)

127 roll film (42 x 42mm)

120 roll film (6 x 6cm)

120 double perforated (6 x 6cm)

120 (6 x 7cm)

Film speed

The term speed describes how light-sensitive film is. A 'fast' film reacts very fast to light, a 'slow' film is less sensitive so needs brighter light or a much longer exposure. Different film speeds cater for different types of photography. A medium speed film is suitable for general everyday pictures; fast film is used in low light conditions or for moving subjects; slow films are used where very fine detail is required. Check carefully what range of film speeds is available for your camera. There is a wide range of different films available for 35mm cameras while 110 film is generally available only in medium and fast speeds.

Why photographs look grainy

Light-sensitive film carries millions of silver halide crystals and it is the size and number of these crystals that determine the speed of the film. The crystals—or grains—on fast film are much larger than those on slow film, which means the print or transparency will look 'grainy'—as though printed on sandpaper. With smaller prints the effect is not very noticeable, but the more a print or slide is enlarged, the more the grain shows up.

Colour film works the same way as black and white film although the effect is often less noticeable because most colour materials are slower.

Speed ratings

Film packs are usually marked with two speed ratings—ISO/ASA (International/American) and DIN (German). The table, right, shows equivalent ASA and DIN speeds. With ASA the doubling of speed is shown by the doubling of the number; with the DIN system the doubling of speed is shown by an increase of 3. For example, 400 ASA film needs only a quarter of the light needed by 100 ASA film.

Ratings for colour and black and white film differ slightly: see chart below.

COLOUR	ASA/DIN	B&W	ASA/DIN
Slow	25/15		(none)
	32/16		32/16
	64/19	Slow	64/19
Medium	80/20		80/20
	100/21		100/21
	125/22	Medium	125/22
	160/23		160/23
Fast	200/24		200/24
	400/27	Fast	400/27

Medium speed film

This is the best general-purpose film for most everyday subjects. It is sensible to get used to using one particular film before experimenting with either slower or faster films. Medium speed films give a useful compromise between speed and grain, and negatives enlarge up to about eight times the dimensions of the negative

▲ Slow films are used in good lighting conditions, especially when slow shutter speeds are possible. These films produce a fine-grained image with plenty of detail and contrast. A slow colour film like Kodachrome 25 (ASA 25) used here, gives a bright, crisp image with fine detail.

▶ Fast films are used in poor lighting conditions or when fast shutter speeds are needed to stop movement. The faster the film the coarser the grain. This enlargement from part of a 35mm negative on a 400 ASA film shows how image quality suffers on fast films.

Fast films

These are for use in low light conditions either indoors, early evening or on dull winter days. Fast films can generally handle most subjects either where the light is bad or where a fast shutter speed is necessary to stop movement. But higher film speed means that pictures look grainy if the negative is enlarged more than about eight times, and there may be some loss of detail.

Even faster black and white films are available and are covered in a later article on Specialist Films.

Slow films

Slow film gives sharp detail and a fine grain-free image, and is therefore particularly useful for big enlargements. It is really best for static subjects such as landscapes, buildings, or still life. Remember that a slow film needs longer exposure time, which increases the risk of camera shake, so these films are often used with the camera on a tripod.

Setting the film speed dial

On cameras that have some form of automatic exposure control you should set the speed rating of the film you are using on the film speed dial. Check this each time you load a new film.

Some 110 cameras are designed to take either 100 ASA cartridge or the faster 400 ASA film, and the camera automatically adjusts the shutter speed as the faster film cartridge is inserted.

▶ The film speed dial must be set to the ASA rating of the film on cameras with automatic exposure control.

▼ The coarser grain quality of a fast film used in poor light need not be a drawback: but in this sunset shot the grain adds to the misty atmosphere.

Filters for colour

Filters for colour give the photographer some measure of control over the final quality of his picture. He can cut through haze, or make colours more realistic by adjusting for excess blue or red light at certain times of day. Filters are amongst the cheapest accessories you can buy and will last for years if you look after them.

Colourless filters

Possibly the most useful filters of all are those which can be used with either black and white or colour film.

Ultra-violet filters absorb UV radiation and therefore effectively reduce haze. On black and white film this adds detail to distant mountains, for example, and on colour film it reduces the haze common in landscape photographs. This filter has little visual effect beyond holding back unwanted ultra-violet light. So it can be left on the lens to protect it from dirt and scratches.

Skylight filters are similar to UV filters. They are widely used and perform several functions. They absorb some ultra-violet light, a major cause of haze and excessive bluishness. But, unlike UV filters, they are slightly pink and come in different densities. Like UV filters, they can be left on the lens all the time.

Neutral density filters don't affect either colour balance or contrast but simply reduce the light entering the lens. They are useful when a camera loaded with fast film is suddenly used to photograph a brightly lit scene, or if shooting at full aperture to give shallow depth of field and the available shutter speed isn't fast enough to prevent over-exposure.

Polarizing filters also act as neutral density filters, reducing the light entering the lens by as much as $1\frac{1}{2}$ to 2 stops, but they do much more than this. They help eliminate glare (reflected light) from surfaces such as windows and water, and the blueness one associates with distant views. The filter also darkens a blue sky if used at right-angles to the sun. Rotate the filter while looking through it until you get the effect you want.

Creative effects

Beyond the purely technical considerations governing their use, filters can be employed to achieve specific creative

▶ **The sea in the background is made distinct from the sky by using a skylight filter to reduce haze.**

◄ A polarizing filter, used at right angles to the sun, increases the blueness of the sky. A distant horizon has greater contrast and appears more distinct. The sky and background (below), photographed without a filter, appear lighter.

► A neutral density filter effectively reduces the light entering the camera. It does not affect the colour or contrast but simply has the effect of down-rating the film speed. This in turn gives a smaller depth of field which means a subject can be made distinct against a more out-of-focus background (see right and below).

◄ Coloured filters for black and white photography can be used on colour film. The effects are extremely dramatic and although not natural, do have visual appeal. The red filter produces a fiery sky while the blue filter gives a cold moonlit effect. The branches are silhouetted against the strong colours of the sky.

▼ The angle of the sun is such that the polarizing filter has no effect on the sky (top left). But the sunlight creates highlights on the water and a polarizing filter is needed to reduce the reflections. A UV and skylight filter would not have any effect on the reflections as they only reduce haze and ultra-violet light.

◀ A polarizing filter reduces the light reflected from glass, making it possible to photograph the driver through the window. The polarizing filter has the same effect on all non-metallic surfaces. This makes it possible to photograph into water, for example, to get a detail of the bottom of a clear stream or fish and plants in the water.

effects. Such use is entirely at the discretion of the photographer and is not subject to hard and fast rules.

Filter ranges include specially designed colour filters to produce pastel or sepia tones with colour film, but any colour filter can be used in conjunction with colour film for a greater variety of effects and moods as shown later in this chapter.

Fluorescent lighting

Tube lighting usually renders natural colour tones incorrectly. With most fluorescent tubes colours tend to be tinged with green. It is difficult to overcome this as different types of tube vary in their colour. As a general guide, with 'daylight' tubes (bluish) use daylight type film; with all other tubes use tungsten type film. Filters are available to correct certain combinations of tube lighting. But for best results, avoid this lighting.

Tungsten lighting

Domestic light bulbs give a warm orange cast to colour slides, and can make the shadows in colour prints look purplish. Colour negative film can usually handle the warmer colour light if you give an extra stop of exposure (change the rating of an ASA 200 film to ASA 100, for example). Colour slide film can not do this and needs a D to A filter, Type 80B, for partial correction. This medium blue filter will still leave the picture slightly warm, which looks natural. Ciné and photo-flood lamps give correct colours when used with this filter, which can be placed in front of the light instead of over the lens, so that daylight and tungsten may be mixed in one shot.

◀ Fluorescent lighting produces a colour cast on colour films. The resulting photographs usually have a greenish tinge. For warm white fluorescent lighting use an FL-D filter to correct the colour cast for more natural looking results.

▶ Different combinations of fluorescent lighting produce different colour casts. If using daylight type film and the light source is daylight type fluorescent use an FL-Day filter to correct the colour.

Filters for effect

Recently photographers have started using many more special effects in their photographs, and there has been a boom in the manufacturing of unusual but simple attachments to produce all sorts of images. Any amateur can, without spending much, match the creative armoury which once cost the professional a large sum. Starbursts, colourful rainbows, rotating prisms, superimposed images, and soft dream effects, are all available to the amateur. The big change has come, in the case of 35mm SLRs, with the multi-purpose filter holder. These attachments screw or push on to the lens, and gelatin, plastic or glass squares are slotted in.

Mounted filters At one time, each round attachment was a glass disc individually mounted in a metal rim, and only one could be screwed on to a lens at any one time. Separately mounted filters are still available, though the very expensive ones, which are used to produce special effects, have been superseded by the multi-purpose filter holder systems.

Step-up/down rings adapt round mounted filters to lenses with a different thread size. This makes it possible to fit filters from independent manufacturers on to most lenses.

How a filter holder works

Unlike round mounted filters, square filters can be placed in their holder at any angle, and the holder can usually be rotated without unscrewing it from the lens rim. The square filters can also be slid up and down freely. Two filters can be sandwiched in one holder or, in the case of the Cokin holder, two slots are provided so that more than one can be used at a time.

In front of this holder, which would be very exposed if left on its own, a lens hood is fitted to shield the filter and lens from direct sun which might cause flare patches or poor contrast in the final picture.

A holder and hood are often combined but detachable. Makes include Hoya (technical filter holder), Cokin (filter systems, holder and hood).

Filter effects

There are several types of special filter available, all creating different effects. **Starbursts** are line ruled filters. They are made by scratching fine lines on a glass or plastic filter, which then produce stars or bursts of light from any point source, such as a street light. Deeper scratches produce stronger effects, and so do more frequent scratches. Very deep rulings may spoil sharpness and closely covered filters, heavily ruled, diffuse the image and give odd colours to the light bursts. Types available include cross-screen (90°), starbursts (60°), and vario-cross (two filters, each parallel ruled, which can be rotated for different angles). There are usually two strengths in any one type of filter. They are generally made in circular mounts and can be rotated. Light burst filters for the Cokin system use irregular scratches instead of line ruling.

Diffraction filters are made by ruling lines far closer together, so finely that the eye cannot tell they are lines. This produces coloured rainbows instead of light bursts, using diffraction to split the light into its colour spectrum elements. Diffraction filters are available in various forms with many effects ranging from a simple line of colour from a light source to a whole array of coloured blobs appearing

▲ A filter holder holds gelatin, glass or plastic squares flat and in position in front of the camera lens. The filter is simply sandwiched between the two sections of the holder. A lens hood can be used in conjunction with a filter holder.

▶ Diffraction filters split light into its colour spectrum elements. They are best used on scenes that have small light points against a dark background.
Paul Constancio

LENS HOODS

metal

rubber

Step-up
step-down
rings

Mounted filter

Square filters

Adapter

Filter holder

Hood

▲ Step-up/down rings adapt round filters to lenses with a different thread size, for example a 52mm filter can be adapted to a 49mm lens or vice versa. Lens hoods can be of metal or rubber and either screw on or snap on to the lens. They can be used even when a filter is attached.

▶ The Cokin universal filter holder can be used with lenses which have a screw thread of 49mm to 58mm. An adapter fits the holder to the lens. The holder takes round and square filters and more than one filter can be used at a time.

▼ 1 A split-field lens has a close-up lens in one half and the other is clear.
2 A soft focus filter diffuses light and creates a soft image.
3 Starburst filters are etched with lines which create patterns on light sources.
4 A centre focus lens is a close-up lens with a hole in the middle.

FILTERS FOR EFFECT

Starburst filters give light sources star shapes. The number of points depend on the pattern of lines on the filter. They can be 4, 6, 8 or multi-burst and each one has its particular use. Two very different uses are shown here.

▶ A multi-burst filter gives the only light source a radiating effect—if there were more light sources the effect would be distracting rather than creative.
Jill Richards

▼ Each light source is broken into 8 points and this regular pattern enhances the lines of lights as they converge on the central image.

▲ A diffraction filter gives the rays of light shining in through the window a touch of colour. The effect is much softer and more natural than diffraction of small strong light sources.
Peter Goodliffe

◄ Far left: without a filter colours appear naturally. Left: adding a fog filter makes the scene become misty and generally more atmospheric without looking contrived.
Lisa le Guay

round a source. The heavier the effect, the more diffusion and unsharpness is introduced. Filters mounted for the camera are normally produced using plastic diffraction sheets mounted on glass. Loose plastic sheets can be bought far more cheaply—these are very fragile but perfectly acceptable for experimenting.

Fog filters do just what they say—they make the picture look as if it has been taken through fog or mist. Unlike real fog, they do not have more effect on distant parts of the picture than near ones, but the effect is still realistic. Fog filters are misty-white to look at, but almost clear to look through, because they have the effect of scattering light passing through them. In darkness, they have no opacity and are, in theory, quite clear. Only when you let light fall on them is there any light to scatter inside them. They do not affect picture sharpness. There are four strengths: pastel, fog no.1, no.2, no.3. The most useful ones are the first three. Fog filters are available in mounted discs and acrylic squares.

Centre focus lenses, also called 'spot' lenses, consist of a dioptric lens (usually +3) with a hole through the middle, so that the edges of the photograph are focused at about 30cm while the main central image is at infinity (dioptric lenses reduce the focusing distance). These lenses are deliberately incapable of making the edge sharp. The result is a sharp central image with blurred edges—suitable for eliminating distracting city backgrounds, for example. These lenses are made in circular mounts.

Sandgrain filters are made by sandblasting or etching the outer edges of a plain glass filter. The outside of the image can then be made not only to blur, but also to fade to grey.

To make a 'misty'

Mistys are made by smearing petroleum jelly on the edges of a clear sheet of plastic in a pattern which surrounds the subject but does not interfere with it. The diffusion is very strong but can be controlled and made to follow the lines of the image. This can be done on a plain glass filter—for example, a UV filter—but with less control. It is best to use a clear plastic sheet inserted in the front of a lens hood. Never, of course, attempt smearing material on the lens itself.

◀ A soft focus filter gives an overall diffused quality to the picture.

▶ A centre focus filter keeps the image in focus at the centre but the surroundings and the background are put out of focus. This is particularly useful for losing distracting backgrounds when photographing portraits in cluttered surroundings.

▶ (Below) A misty is made by spreading vaseline on a clear glass filter, such as a UV filter, which then softens the image.

▼ A split-field lens with a close-up lens on one half focuses on the foreground while the other half allows the lens to focus normally at infinity for a distant subject.

Soft focus filters, also called diffusers, have fine lines etched on the filter which softens the edges of the picture but leaves the centre sharp. Filters for an overall soft focus effect are also available. These filters are particularly suitable for portraits as skin blemishes become less obvious.

Split-field lenses are made by cutting a close-up lens in half, which results in a split field. This allows one half of the lens to focus on a close distance while the other half is on a distant subject. The filter can be rotated to move the division round, and in square moulded form can slide up and down in the holder to adjust the division ratio. Split-field lenses are made to achieve a sharp image, unlike centre focus lenses. The camera lens must be used quite wide open to prevent sharp distinction between the two planes of focus appearing in the middle of the picture.

Special effects using colour filters can add interest to an otherwise dull scene. To be successful these filters should be used with discretion; scenes low in colour or contrast, for example, lend themselves to added colour. The colour can be added in different ways depending on the particular colour and type of filter being used.

These filters can be used in combination with the special effects filters discussed previously. Shoot a roll of film with the various filters and keep a record so that you can repeat successes.

This is also particularly useful if you do not have through-the-lens metering, in which case exposure must be increased according to the filter factor. Whatever filter you use don't overdo it. A starburst in every one of your holiday photographs will ruin the whole effect; orange tints on all landscapes become boring, as do endless photographs that look as though flooded with moonlight. Be discerning in the use of filters—use them where they are visually creative and not just for the sake of being different.

Split colour filters have one half of one colour and the other of a different colour. They can also be divided into three colours. The idea of these is to add dramatic colours in strong divisions to ordinary subjects. They can be difficult to use successfully. The made-up filters, in normal mounts, have colours which are carefully balanced in density so that one does not affect the exposure more than the other. You can also make your own by buying filter acetates or gelatin and taping them together to fit into a filter holder.

▲ A combination of filters was used for this shot. A soft focus filter diffuses the overall image and a split colour filter, one half red and the other half blue, adds dramatic colour.

A graduated filter has one side clear and the other coloured. A split colour filter combines two different colours.

Graduated filters are clear on one half, with a diffused dividing line in the middle, turning to a neutral grey or a coloured half. They are also known as 'graduates' or 'chromos'. They are used where one half of a scene—normally the sky—is too bright, and positioned so that the coloured half covers the bright area and the clear half allows the darker part of the scene to come through at full brightness. They can be used to correct, as when using a grey filter to darken a bright sky; to enhance, as when using a blue filter to make a dull white sky look blue; and to produce effects, as when turning a sky red or the sea green, or imitating a sunset. They are available as round mounted filters (Hoya, Cromofilter, Lee, Vivitar Halfchrome) and as square acrylic ones (Cokin).

FILTERS FOR EFFECT

Pastels and sepia effects can be achieved by using coloured filters. These filters are lightly coloured and allow the subject colours to show through that of the filter. They can be used very effectively in conjunction with soft focus filters, or diffusers. Another successful way to use them is to combine a sepia filter with a 'misty'. The effect of this is to soften the outer edges of the picture and can be very atmospheric.

▲ A gelatin filter is sandwiched in a mount to keep it flat inside the holder. Square glass filters do not need mounting—they slot directly into the filter holder on the camera.

▶ A fog filter and a violet filter were used together to soften the image and add a hint of colour to the scene.
Lisa le Guay

▲ A coastal scene photographed without a filter produces normal colour tones.

▲ A pink filter completely changes the colour and mood of the scene to a monochrome image.

▲ A sepia filter reduces some of the colour in the scene to create a slightly sombre picture.

Pure colour filters are produced in very strong colours such as blue, purple, orange or red. They can be used with colour film to give an overall hue with high contrast. Red, blue or yellow filters expose only one emulsion layer and may give a stark effect; secondary colours like purple are richer. Even with a dense filter, bright light sources may 'burn through' to produce white on the film with adequate exposure.

▼ Colour filters can be round or square and some have a clear centre spot for a special effect.

▲ A graduated filter adds a warm tint to this misty scene. Without the filter the picture would have been almost without colour, with the reflected image simply being a repeat of the subject.
Martin Riedl

◄ The same scene shot with various filters produces different results. A starburst filter breaks the light source into eight points. A split colour filter, used in conjunction with the starburst filter retains the star-shaped light source and adds blue and red to the sky.
David Morey

The image on a film is formed by a lens which has been designed very carefully to produce an exact picture of the scene it is focused on. But it is possible to form a coherent clear image on the film which does not resemble the original scene. Extra optical attachments which change the path of the light rays coming through the lens, but still bring them into focus can repeat, split, blur, colour, bend or fracture the image in many ways. There are various gadgets which can be used to create unfamiliar perspectives on the world seen by the camera. Distortion is possible, just as it is with fairground mirrors.

Many of the devices which are normally sold as filters for lens mountings or to slot into filter systems fall into this category of optical effects rather than filters and certainly do not 'filter' the light. However, they are often referred to as 'special effects filters' because the word has come to be used to describe anything which fits in front of a lens. These filters can be used in combinations—for example, a colour filter can be used with a multi-image filter.

Multi-image filters

These are thick optical glass discs cut as prismatic facets which split the image into repeated, overlapping images. Many different types are available. The simplest ones repeat the image three times, side by side; more popular ones give a sharp central normal image surrounded by three, four, five, or six repeat images which are less crisp and contrasty than the central image.

Repeater or echo prisms use three or six facets cut very close together to give a series of parallel images tailing away from the main subject.

Colour prisms have each facet coloured differently, so that overlapping coloured versions of the main picture are produced. These are expensive, but you can make a temporary colour prism by colouring a plain prism with a felt tip pen.

By putting a much thicker prism at an angle in front of the lens, you can produce an elongated or colour-fringed image – the effect is similar to looking through cut glass at a light, without clearly repeated images. This can be done by holding some normal multi-image prisms at an angle or by buying a special colour fringe prism such as the one available in the Cokin system. Any laboratory prism, if you can get hold of one, can be used to experiment with.

▲ A filter with three parallel facets (left) repeats the image three times. The filter can be rotated on the lens to change the direction of the repeated images.

◄ A filter with three facets (above) repeats the images at random. *Derek Bayes*

► Six parallel facets on one half of a filter (above) gives an added effect of movement.

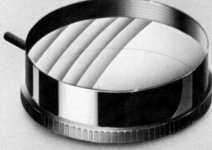

The picture

The camera is a window through which you view the world; the shutter release lets you freeze an instant from this moving image permanently. Composing your image and timing the moment so that all the elements combine harmoniously is the essence of photo vision.

Composition is not something which comes naturally, even if you have an excellent sense of balance, shape and form. The fixed rectangle of the viewfinder, and later on the slide or print, is a highly selective frame. Unlike the artist who can omit or enhance, the photographer has to accept the real world. Viewpoint and perspective become important. Colours dominate, and control how the elements in the picture are emphasized. The three-dimensional world becomes a flat plane of patterns, lines, and tones which the eye uses to reconstruct reality.

Enough pictures have been taken for successful ideas to be identified and explained, and ways of seeing and composing the picture to be taught in straightforward language. No-one can become a great natural photographer by studying successful pictures, but everyone can improve their own pictures this way.

Why take the picture?

One of the main reasons that people are often disappointed with their pictures is simply because they don't ask themselves why they wanted to take them in the first place.

The simple answer, of course, is that a particular scene was attractive. But in what way? While you are actually taking the picture the important thing is to know why you want to record it, and what exactly it is about the subject that makes you feel that way.

The centre of interest

If the subject is a landscape, for example, is it the line of distant hills that pleases you? Or perhaps the effect of the sunlight on the trees? Alternatively, are you attracted by the cloud formation? What is it, in fact, that you are going to make the centre of interest in your picture?

Until you become aware of exactly what it is that is attracting your attention you cannot begin to know how to go about photographing it. You also need to understand your reason for wanting to record it. Is it, for example,

the mood of the situation you wish to capture or the geographical details of the landscape? If you wanted to take a picture of your house to help sell it you would almost certainly approach the problem in a quite different way from that of a picture which was going to support a claim for a reduction in the rates. The same sort of reasoning should lie behind every picture you take.

To return to the example of the landscape. A picture intended to convey the mood of the scene may well require the sunlight and the sky to be of prime importance; the other details will be of less concern. For an accurate record shot on the other hand the atmosphere may well have to be sacrificed in order to get the maximum detail and gradation in the landscape itself.

Seeing the subject

Once you have established your reasons for shooting the picture you need to decide which of the components of the scene will help you

produce the best and most effective result.

To do this you must learn to look objectively at your subject. You must, in fact, learn to be able to see like a camera.

The human eye is an incredible piece of optical equipment. Often, however, other senses over-ride what the eye registers and it can be very easy to look at a scene without really seeing it clearly. Your general impression is just as likely to be influenced by your mood and by sounds and smells, and even memories, as it is by purely visual information. The camera lens, however, is not affected by anything other than the visual content of the scene, which it will record quite objectively.

In a landscape scene, for example, not only will the camera fail to record the smell of newly mown hay and the warmth of the sun, but it will also seek out unpleasant things like barbed wire fences and rusty tin sheds which your eyes have glossed over. In fact, the whole scene may well appear quite differently.

A common fault with many photographs is that they are taken too far away from the subject and from the wrong angle. Often, too, the background becomes confused with the main subject. All these criticisms apply to the photograph below. The flamingo has its back turned and the background is neither sharp enough to show detail nor blurred enough to be unobtrusive. A much stronger shot would have been a close—up, like that on the right, taken with a longer focus lens. If you don't have a long lens, spend more time choosing your viewpoint for an overall shot. Compare the picture below with that far right, where selective focusing and careful choice of viewpoint have made a bold, simple image.

How we react to colour

Another reason for taking photographs is to capture on film the wealth of colour around us. The way colour is used greatly influences the mood of a picture and is an important element of composition.

Colour plays a large part in our feelings towards what we see. Most of our reactions towards individual colours stem originally from their use in nature. Learning about colour is therefore really only a question of looking around.

You will notice, for example, that red stands out and commands attention in much the same way as a strong highlight in a black and white photograph. This is because red is an aggressive colour, and is used in nature either to attract attention or to signify danger. Blue and green, however, are more subdued. They are the predominant colours in a summer landscape and are associated with feelings of peace.

Similarly, most people regard colours as being either hot or cold. Orange, yellow and red are associated with fire, the sun and hot weather and are therefore thought of as hot colours, while blue tends to be associated with water, snow and ice and is considered chilly.

Another factor affecting the mood evoked is the strength of a colour. Soft colours evoke the feeling of romance, while dark colours are sombre and mysterious.

Colour to emphasize mood

The more you actually look at colour, rather than just accepting it as part of the scenery, the greater will be your understanding of the response it produces. You can then use it to emphasize the mood of your pictures. The dreariness of grey city buildings can be heightened by a bright flower poking out of a crack in the pavement. However, a larger area of bright colour would

◀ In this scene *Michael Busselle* was attracted by the group of figures and the relationship between the colours of their clothing and those of the poster above. By going in close he has managed to convey this quite clearly. The picture below, however, leaves some doubt as to the main area of interest. To create impact it is usually best to keep the image simple.

▶ An attractive scene is often not enough to make a really striking photograph. The picture on the right is pretty, but unexceptional. The picture below works much better because the splash of red is so unexpected compared with the gentleness of the rest of the composition.

detract from the overall mood.

So it is vital to look carefully at the colours in the scene you wish to photograph. Single out each of the colours, be aware of where each is in relation to the others and judge which contribute most to the mood you want to capture or evoke ánd which detract. The overall colour impression of the scene is very important.

There are also artificial ways of creating mood. Slight over-exposure makes colours appear weaker, and soft focusing and fog filters subdue strong colours, lending an air of dreaminess to your subject. Extra control can be exercised by using colour filters. These and other methods are covered in the chapter on colour.

▶ **Many of our reactions towards colour stem originally from how it is used in nature. Red, orange and yellow are generally regarded as being hot, and we feel the heat of a picture when these colours are included. In nature they are the colours of the sun and are beautifully captured here by *Alex Langley*, conveying the tropical atmosphere surrounding a mosque in Borneo.**

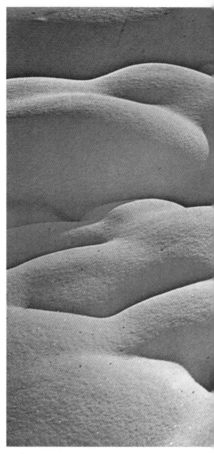

▲ The blue cast in the shadow areas of this picture has been caused by reflections from a blue sky. Snow and ice frequently have this quality and it is because of these wintry associations that we regard blue as a cold colour. Using 64 ASA film, the exposure of 1/125 at f11 was calculated to retain detail in the high-light areas. *Ernst Haas*

◀ Careful selection of view-point has ensured that distracting areas of colour, which might have disturbed the gentle mood, have been excluded from this picture.

▶ A conflict of mood has resulted in this picture, taken by *Suzanne Hill* on a lake in Kashmir. Although the gaiety of the flowers dominates the composition, the darkness of the water has a more sombre feeling. You can almost imagine a coffin in the boat.

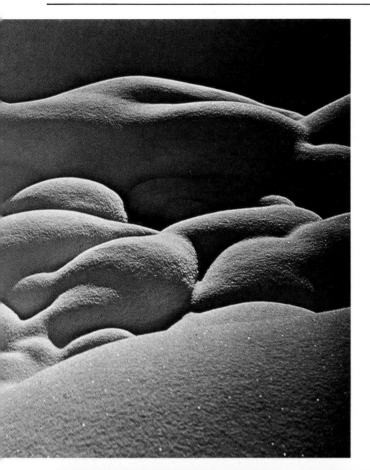

▲ To create the appropriate mood for this picture, *John Garrett* has kept plenty of space around the subject. Slight under-exposure has brightened the colour of the robes, but the grey impression of the background dominates the mood.

The viewfinder

The panoramic view on the right is very much as the eye sees it—but the eye will subconsciously focus on certain details as it moves across the landscape. What each person notices is very much a personal choice—it may be the form of a particular tree, the pattern made by branches or the position of a figure.

When you take a photograph you make two decisions: *what* you are going to include and *when* to press the button. In both instances you need to consider how to show the subject in the most effective way.

Good composition may mean simplifying your photograph by changing viewpoint—moving higher, lower, more to one side. It certainly means thinking about the direction and quality of the lighting. This can make all the difference between a photograph which is muddled or boring, and one which looks right.

How to 'see' better pictures

Some people have a natural ability to see a composition right away—but most of us have to keep looking, experimenting, and looking again, until we start seeing well composed photographs. But remember, this is something anyone can do, no matter how simple or elaborate their camera.

Photography is concerned with seeing the world in terms of how it appears in a rectangular (or square) shape on a flat piece of paper. The question is, which parts of what you see should the camera include . . . or leave out? This depends not only on the main centre of interest but also on the visual appeal of shapes, colours, patterns, and textures. Moving around, looking through the viewfinder, helps you emphasize important aspects and isolate them from the overall view. Look also at the way objects may be cut by the edges of your picture. The hard lines at the edges of the viewfinder give a definite border to what you select. You might cut off a vital part of the subject by mistake—or use this border to contain the picture. This is another difference between seeing the scene as the human eye sees it and composing it into a photograph.

To become more aware of composition it is helpful to make a cardboard viewing frame. Look through it at familiar objects, parts of your home, people's faces or landscapes. It is surprising how, by imposing this frame on what you see, you start to discover interesting 'pictures' where you may not have noticed them before.

▶ With a camera the photographer can choose which part of the general view becomes the subject and a static scene, such as a landscape, gives time for careful composition in the viewfinder. Experiment by changing the camera position and moving in closer on parts of the scene to find out how this affects what you see in the viewfinder. Introducing figures into a landscape gives an immediate sense of scale and often contributes to the balance and interest of the composition.

▶ Centre: picking out a detail may say as much about a scene as the larger view. In a woodland the fresh green of leaves in spring create an unforgettable image, so why not go right in and capture that quality by filling the viewfinder entirely. The skill comes in *seeing* the detail and then isolating it from the overall view.

▼ Tall, slim trees just ask for a vertical format. By moving in close this picture emphasizes the soaring quality of the trees; patterns of light and shade; rough texture of bark against a lacy canopy of leaves. You can strengthen the vertical shape later by cutting the print—known as cropping—to make a narrower shape than the film format.

Using a viewfinder

Some people find the camera view-finder rather awkward and inhibiting—a mechanical block between them and the subject. This is where a cardboard viewing frame is useful. It helps to train the eye to see and compose successful pictures.

Whether you use a frame, or the camera itself, this section is concerned with exploring the effects of changing viewpoint. Even though you will usually be composing far more complicated pictures of groups of people, interiors, or landscapes it is well worth starting by looking at just one simple object and *seeing* it. Here you are dealing with three main elements: a) the subject, b) the rectangle or square imposed by the picture format, and c) the spaces around the subject.

As you look at the subject, notice how important the spaces around it are—both the shapes they make and the way the shadow falls. The strength, position and shape of the shadow help to define the subject's three–dimensional form.

What subject to choose?

This will depend on how close your camera lens can get to the subject—check the minimum focusing distance of your camera, then pick something that fills the viewfinder. If you can get as close as 45cm you might choose a china cup and saucer. If your minimum distance is about 90cm then choose something larger with an interesting shape, such as a chair or a watering can.

LONG VIEW
Start by looking at the subject from as far away as possible. Now move in, seeing how the subject looks on the right of the viewing frame, then on the left. In each case, is your eye led into, or out of, the frame?

CLOSE UP
Move in close until the subject fills the frame (try this out with both formats). The closer you get the more you become aware of the shape of the background, and how light and shadow give form to the subject.

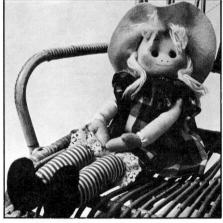

DETAIL
Even if your camera lens does not let you get closer than 90cm, take a look at details through the viewing frame—the close–up view may be more intriguing and interesting lines, textures and patterns may emerge.

If you try this out using film, aim to have a neutral background, which does not interfere with the shape of the subject. You may be able to isolate the subject from distracting surroundings on a large piece of paper, in an empty room or passage, on a white sheet, or in the middle of a lawn. Position the subject and yourself so that the daylight lights the subject from the side. (Don't use flash as you cannot be sure what effect it will create.) With a simple subject like a chair, you have two choices—either to move the subject, or to move the camera. It's a good idea to get into the habit of moving the camera rather than the subject so that when you come to an immovable object, such as a tree you are used to moving around to find the best viewpoint.

The viewing frame

A colour–slide mount will do, but a larger, black cardboard frame helps to isolate the subject far better. You need a steel ruler, a sheet of matt black cardboard, about 30 x 23cm, a craft knife and a pencil.
Draw a rectangle in the proportion of 2:3, such as 4 x 6cm, and a square about 2 x 2cm, and cut out. Work on the black side to keep the edges crisp.

With the black side facing you, close one eye and look through the frame. Move it towards and away from you until the subject is framed in a pleasing way. Everyday objects can make effective pictures when they are cleverly positioned and background clutter is cut out.

Using the format

Basically, there are two photographic formats: square and rectangular. The size of the rectangle varies, but the proportion of 2:3 is generally appropriate for 110 and 35mm film. With a viewing frame in both shapes you can compare the effect of using the two formats—a useful point to consider when you buy a new camera. Some people are devoted to one format and find it hard to work with the other. Start by looking at the subject from the same viewpoint through one and then the other format and, of course, try the rectangle both horizontally and vertically.

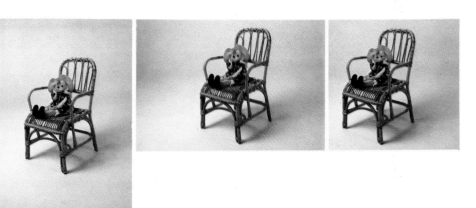

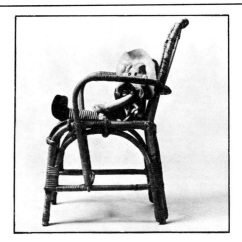

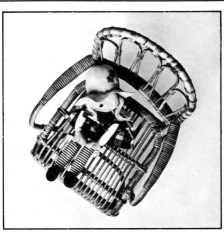

LOW LEVEL VIEW
Now try a lower viewpoint: does the subject look most effective from ground level, or a little higher? Is the subject identifiable, or do you need to move around to find a better vantage point?

FROM ABOVE
With a plan view of the subject the shapes of the horizontal parts become important and the surface it stands on forms the background. A truly 'over the top' view often simplifies shapes and lines.

SILHOUETTE
Move directly opposite the light source, then adjust the viewing height until you achieve the most satisfactory silhouette. For a clear, clean shape the horizontal lines of the subject should suggest the correct height.

Seeing in colour

The vocabulary of colour
When considering the effects of colour it is useful to know a little about why colours react with each other in the way that they do. Why, for example, does a green leaf look different when viewed in turn against a white wall, a blue sky and a red flower?

How colours react together
There are three basic ways in which colours react with each other: they either contrast, harmonize or clash and are discordant. These reactions are, to some extent, due to their position on the spectrum.

The colour wheel shown here is a simplified version of the spectrum, bent into a circle. From it you will see that those colours which tend to harmonize are close to each other and those which contrast—red and green, for example—are well apart. The other two wheels separate the primary from the secondary, or complementary, colours.

You will see that the primary colours of light differ from those of paint. Note that the colours of both wheels contrast, the primaries more sharply than the secondaries.

The green leaf, therefore, is seen most naturally when viewed against the neutral background of a white wall. It will, however, harmonize with the blue of the sky, appearing softer and more gentle, and contrast with the red flower, which will make it appear harsher and more aggressive.

Types of colour
Although the reasons for harmony, contrast and discord given here are generally true, you will find that at times—maybe on a hazy day—colours that would normally contrast appear to be in harmony. This is because the strength and brilliance of the colours are reduced and therefore more in accord, even if the colours themselves are not.

This strength of colour depends upon three factors: hue (basic colour), saturation (purity) and brightness (reflected light).

● It is the **hue** which distinguishes one colour from another—blue from red, for example.

● The **saturation** is the purity of hue. The hues in the colour wheels are fully saturated, pure colour. They become desaturated by the addition of either black (shadow) or white (light), white producing a tint and black giving a shade. (See diagram, centre right.)

● The **brightness** of a colour depends upon the amount of light reflected by the hue; yellow, for instance, is naturally bright, blue less so, and tints are brighter than shades.

Therefore, on a hazy day the light desaturates colour, the qualities are consequently weakened and harmony is more likely to be produced from contrast or discord. A very bright day can also have a similar effect. The strong light induces glare, is bounced off reflective surfaces and the colours of the subject become desaturated.

The pictures below and right illustrate the terms which will be used in the pages on colour which follow. Each aspect of colour will be dealt with in turn: the term will be defined and explained more fully, and guidelines will be given on the best way to make use of each when composing colour photographs. By the end of the chapter you should

find that colour awareness comes more naturally to you. However, if at any time you feel you need reminding of what you should be looking for when you have a colour film in your camera, you can refer back to these pages and use them as a guide. These images have been chosen because they illustrate each point in the most simple way and are easy to remember.

▶ **This chart demonstrates the principle of desaturation. The fully saturated band in the middle is seen in perfect lighting conditions. The desaturated areas (tints and shades) on either side are created by adverse light: bright light in the case of tints, and weak light or shadow in the case of shades.**

Colour as the subject

Colour contrast

Colour harmony

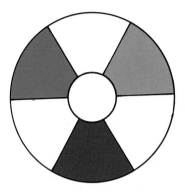

Red, blue and green are the *primary colours* of light. They differ from the primary colours of pigment (red, blue and yellow) but like pigment primaries they can be mixed to produce any hue.

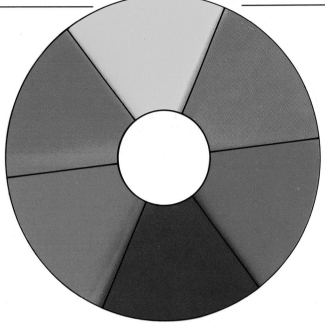

THE COLOUR WHEEL

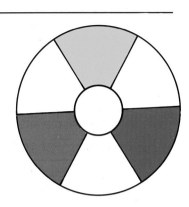

The *complementary colours* of light are formed from a combination of two primaries. Magenta is formed from a mixture of red and blue, yellow from red and green and cyan from green and blue.

Accent colour

Monochromatic

Polychromatic

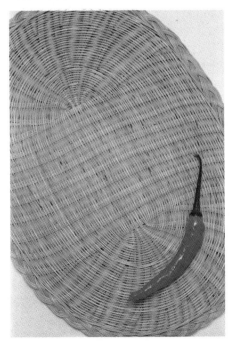

Where to put the subject

To many experienced photographers deciding where to put the subject in the viewfinder is instinctive. But for the beginner it needs as much attention as the horizon, the background or the foreground. Guidelines are useful for beginners, but you should soon start to let yourself react to the subject and not feel inhibited by rules.

The most obvious placing for the subject is in the centre of the frame: that way there is no danger of cutting off the tops of heads, or other important parts of the scene.

But a centrally placed subject often results in a dull picture. It also means that the photographer may not be filling the frame enough, with the all-too-common result that the subject is too small in the final print and becomes absorbed in a background which adds little to the picture.

However, a centrally placed subject can work particularly well when the picture has strong geometric lines that the photographer wants to capture. This can be especially true when photographing architecture where the geometric balance is important.

Most people find they prefer to look at a point just above the geometric centre, so consider positioning the most important part of the subject just above mid-centre. Then see the effect of moving this part to the geometric centre, to the top half of the picture and then below, and see which is most effective for the particular subject.

▼ The middle of the frame is often the most satisfactory place for a round subject. Here, background would be a distraction from the minute, precise detail. *Eric Crichton*

▶ A strongly geometric composition: oblong door, triangular ladder and the man dead centre, with just the position of his hand and swinging foot to add a touch of vitality. *Martin Parr*

▲ Putting the subject dead centre tends to make it static, while moving it a bit to one side gives the whole picture a more dynamic sense of movement. *Robert Estall*

The intersection of thirds

The traditional way to produce a balanced, satisfying composition is to use the 'intersection of the thirds'. Painters have used this formula for centuries and some photographers find it helpful too. But take care not to apply this rule rigidly to every picture or you will soon find the results boring and repetitive.

If you have a subject such as a tree, or a person, or a chair, start by positioning it on one of the two vertical third lines. This position often gives a more satisfactory composition than a central one. (Compare this with the section on where to put the horizon.)

Next, imagine that the scene is divided into thirds, both horizontally and vertically. The intersection of the thirds produces four 'ideal' points on which to position the subject.

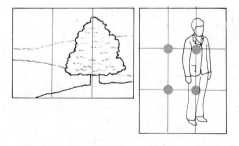

Above left: a diagram showing the positions of the vertical thirds.
Above right: a diagram showing the four 'intersections of thirds'.

▲ All the photographs on these pages are balanced differently to suit either the shape or mood of the particular subjects. Landscapes are the easiest subjects to experiment with because they do not move. This cottage is shown positioned on a vertical third: now consider how the picture would look with the cottage a little higher, or lower, positioned on one of the intersections. *John Bulmer*

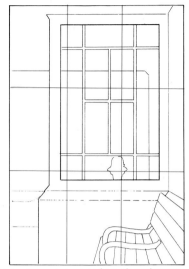

▶ When you are arranging the picture in the viewfinder try altering the camera position. The photographer used the strong rectangular shape of the window to dominate the picture, and the placing of the head—to which the eye is immediately drawn—is balanced by the bench at the bottom of the picture. With a still subject take more than one picture and try arranging the composition differently. *Bryn Campbell*

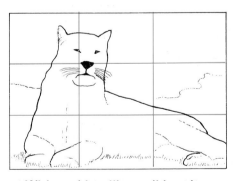

◀ With a subject like a wild cat it is less easy to move the camera. Here, the head and shoulders of the animal dominate the composition. A lower placing of the head would have meant cutting off the bottom of the body — making a weaker picture. *Eric Stoye*

Emphatic alternatives

Placing a subject off-centre in any direction is one of the many ways of creating emphasis in a photograph, making the eye go straight to the subject. At first glance the family group by Tomas Sennett (far right) might seem unbalanced, with the figures squashed right over to the side of the frame. But in fact the group is carefully balanced by the expanse of sea, which also places them in their seaboard surroundings.

Similarly, Roland Michaud's picture of the Tibetan monk—placed firmly to one side of the frame—is a satisfying, well-balanced composition because the face is looking *into* the picture. By closing in on the head, the photographer leaves no doubt where the centre of interest lies.

If you place a subject off centre, what happens to the 'space' created? In many cases, like the two pictures just mentioned, the space becomes a balancing factor in the composition. The photographer can also use the space to add information about the subject.

Room to move

But there is another important reason for not composing certain pictures too tightly. A moving subject seldom looks right if placed in the middle of the frame. Patrick Ward's picture of the man on the bicycle needs the space on the right of the frame. It is not only a question of balance but also that a moving subject needs space to 'move into'. This is especially worth remembering in sports photography, although often difficult to achieve as all one's attention is on the action.

Another effect of leaving plenty of space around the subject is to emphasize loneliness or isolation. Here the space around the subject is as vital as the subject itself. The photograph of the tractor ploughing would have been less effective if it had been taken close to—the space emphasizes the scale of the open landscape.

Try it another way

All this is not to say that every subject should be placed off-centre. The important thing is to try various alternatives before taking the picture. If you can't move the subject move the camera and, if there is time, take more than one picture, varying the camera viewpoint to change the placing of the subject. If you can't move yourself or the subject but can change lenses to alter the angle of view, try using a lens of different focal length.

Emphasis is a way of making people notice a picture they might otherwise not have looked at. There are various ways of achieving this—by the way the picture is composed or by the way shapes, pattern and colour are used. Where the subject is placed is one of the most obvious ways of drawing attention to it. All the photographs on these two pages seem to break the obvious rules—but all succeed in holding our attention.

◄ Emphasizing the sense of wide-open space with a vast sky.

◄ Emphasizing the monk's gaze by leaving space in front of him.

► Emphasizing the importance of the sea in these people's lives.

▼ Emphasizing movement by leaving space for the bicycle to 'move into'.

Frame within a frame

It is not always possible to fill the frame with the main subject of your photograph. Perhaps it is too far away and you have no lens long enough to do away with the empty foreground and blank area of sky behind. Unless you do your own printing and can enlarge the important part of the photograph, it will lose its impact.

One solution to this is to find a viewpoint which gives the subject its own 'frame within a frame'. Not only does this mask the empty foreground and background—or any ugly features that would detract from the picture—but it also has the positive effect of focusing attention on the main point of interest.

Frames for buildings

Photographs of buildings often suffer from this problem. Getting far enough away from the building to include a high turret or to avoid converging verticals may leave you with bleak, unused areas at the edges of the frame. Or your subject may be a beautiful old building surrounded by incongruous modern office blocks which would destroy the character of the shot. In many cases the best 'frame within a frame' for a building is part of another building. Arches, doorways or windows are ideal for the purpose, with shapes that make a positive contribution to the foreground of your shot.

If you are using a doorway or an arch to frame your subject, you will often be photographing from the inside looking out. The interior will be dark compared to the view outside and the frame will appear in silhouette. Areas of strong black in the foreground will

FRAMES FOR BUILDINGS

▲ Though the gold roof of the mosque is effective against the deep blue sky, its shape did not make a strong picture. *A. Evans* solved the problem by moving back and using an arch in the foreground to frame the subject. It echoes the dome of the mosque nicely.

◀ Here the arch leads the eye into the alley, and gives it a secretive, rather mysterious atmosphere. It also adds to the sense of depth. *Malcolm Aird* needed a 35mm wide-angle lens to get it all in. Costa Smeralda, Sardinia.

▶ *Patrick Thurston* found a doorway to frame his shot of Exeter Cathedral. It allowed him to 'lose' unwanted detail and focus attention on the tower. The apparent tilt of the building is matched by the angle of the frame.

intensify the colours within the frame, but the shape of the frame you choose will be all the more important.

Unless you want a very dramatic 'keyhole' effect, a silhouetted frame should occupy only a small area of the picture. But even this small area of black will affect the exposure reading of an averaging TTL meter. So, to make sure of the right effect you should always take your reading from the main subject and then return to the viewpoint that gives you your silhouetted frame. If your camera sets its own exposure automatically, use the manual override or the memory lock.

Trees, wrought iron gates, even statues and or fountains offer frames that can provide foreground interest in a picture of a distant building. Remember, though, that if the frame is not in silhouette, too much bright colour or complicated detail may draw attention away from the main subject. Single colours and simple, predictable shapes are best. If possible choose something that adds to the character of the building.

Frames for people

The 35mm frame is not always best suited to photographing people, particularly when used horizontally. The square format is often worse, with the figure looking dwarfed by the empty areas on either side. Here again, doorways (designed to fit the human form!) and windows make useful frames within frames, modifying the rectangular shape of the frame with another rectangle of different proportions.

If you position the camera square on to the door or window, the symmetrical area around it will give the portrait a rather formal 'border' effect, emphasizing the figure even more. For shots like this choose a frame that fits in with the mood of the picture. You can also help your subject to pose by asking him or her to use the frame as a prop, with a hand on the doorknob or window catch for example.

Look around for frames that will under line the character of the person you want to photograph. Foreground flowers and foliage for a romantic picture—even if you leave them slightly out of focus, making use of the colours alone—or a circular rubber tyre if you are photographing a mechanic at work. The actions or expression of your subject may be no different, but you have added to the viewer's impression of him or her by filling the otherwise redundant area of the frame with extra information.

FRAMES FOR PEOPLE
▲ With one car window open and one closed, *Lawrence Lawry* could put his subject in a frame and at the same time reflect the sunset she was watching.

◄ As well as improving the proportions, each of these doorways suggested a different pose for the portrait. *Anne Conway*

Unusual frames

As well as complementing your subject by your choice of frame, you can also create a strong effect by finding a frame that contrasts with the subject. Old against new, rusty metal against shining steel, a brand-new skyscraper viewed through the broken structure of a derelict building, or an elegant sailing boat framed by the girders of a dockside crane.

When using this approach, a wide angle lens will give you two major advantages. The contrast will work best if the frame is at least partially recognizable, and a wide angle will allow you a greater depth of field to keep both frame and subject in sharp focus. It will also allow you to approach closer to the framing object and incorporate a wider angle of view of the scene beyond.

Mirrors make unusual frames within frames and can create an arresting contrast between the reflection itself and the mirror's surroundings. Try using a mirror with an interesting frame for a portrait of a person or even a curious animal. Or find an angle that will give a surprise view or extra information about the subject—green fields reflected in a factory window, for example.

You can also play tricks with mirrors. If you take a mirror out into the countryside, you can—by hiding the edges of the mirror behind foliage—take pictures of disembodied faces appearing in trees, or hands picking roses from a briar. If you have a reflex camera focusing is no problem. If not, remember that the focusing point is the distance from the camera to the mirror *plus* the distance from the mirror surface to the object reflected.

To sum up

If you look through your viewfinder and discover that, although the subject itself is interesting, the area around it looks blank and unexciting, search around for a 'frame within a frame' to add foreground interest. Frames to watch out for are:
● doors, windows and other architectural structures;
● leaves, branches and flowers;
● fences, gates, statues or fountains;
● industrial machinery;
● mirrors or other reflective surfaces.

▶ **Moving in closer to these chickens would have shown more detail, but by including the whole door above them, *John Garrett* put them in an interesting frame. The symmetrical composition has a decorative appeal.**

▲ **Any reflecting object can be a frame. Here the plaque in one gate also** reflects the other. *Ed Mullis* took the picture outside a palace in Bahrain.

Scale and depth

One of the greatest limitations of photography is that it has to show a three-dimensional subject by using a two-dimensional medium—a piece of photographic paper or film. However, when you look at a photograph you don't usually experience too much difficulty in assessing the depth and form of the objects contained within the picture. This is because there are clues to help you, and one of the most important of these is perspective, and more particularly linear perspective.

It is linear perspective that governs the shape and size of objects in relation to their distance from the point at which they are seen—the viewpoint.

Another aspect of perspective is that which governs the tonal quality of an object in relation to viewpoint. This is known as aerial or atmospheric perspective. However, for the purpose of this chapter, perspective is used to mean

linear perspective.

As a photographer, the more you learn about the tricks of perspective and how to use them the more you can create a sense of dramatic 3-D depth to suit the subject of your pictures.

Converging lines

Everyone knows that if you look down a railway track the rails appear to converge. They get closer and closer together until, at a considerable distance away, they appear to touch. The sleepers also appear to get smaller and closer together. Yet, if you were able to walk along the track with a measure, you would find that the rails were the same distance apart and that the space between the sleepers remained constant, however far down the line you walked. This apparent convergence is due to an effect called perspective—the fact that objects nearest to us always

▲ **The use of converging lines, which the eye accepts as indicating distance, is one of the most simple and effective ways of giving a picture a feeling of depth. By standing in the middle of the road to take this picture** *Steve Herr* **has further dramatized the effect.**

appear larger than identical objects placed further away.

A railway track is a simple and obvious example because we know that the lines are the same distance apart, but the effects of perspective are with us all the time. The buildings seen when looking down a street, even if they are not all identical, appear proportionally narrower and proportionally less deep (smaller) the further they are from the viewer. The brain, however, because it uses previous knowledge and experience, modifies the eyes' accurate image and tells us that the buildings are

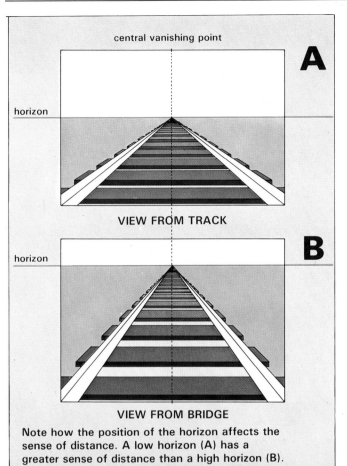

central vanishing point

A

horizon

VIEW FROM TRACK

B

horizon

VIEW FROM BRIDGE

Note how the position of the horizon affects the sense of distance. A low horizon (A) has a greater sense of distance than a high horizon (B).

Including parallel lines which appear to meet in the distance is not in itself enough to make a good picture with plenty of depth. You have to choose a viewpoint from which this aspect of perspective can be best exploited to reflect the mood you wish to convey. *Paolo Koch* chose a low, central viewpoint for the picture of oil pipes in Iran (above), exactly right for a feeling of power and industry.
Lisa Mackson used a high viewpoint to draw the eye down into the quiet seclusion of the woodland scene (left).
John Bulmer stood slightly to one side to lead the eye from the front of the picture to the train (far left), while making the most of the curve at the end of the track.

the same size along the entire length of the street. You may *know* this to be true, but it is not the image received by your eye. Your brain has translated the information and decided to ignore perspective.

So, having established that your brain has been tricking you all your life, as a photographer you must now start trying to see what your eyes actually register. Because the camera does not have a brain, it will not ignore perspective. So learn to rely more upon your eyes and less on previous experience.

Vanishing points

Vanishing points and the horizon are two essential elements of perspective. Taking the railway track as an example again, you can see that the lines appear to converge at a point which is as far as the eye can see, and then disappear. This is the *vanishing point*.

In any one scene there may be more than one vanishing point. If you stand between the rails and look along the track you will see that there is only one, central, vanishing point (see diagram A). However, if you turn your head and look at a building from a corner (diagrams C, D, E and F) there are two, one on either side. Whatever their number, however, and whichever direction you look in, from the same viewpoint all vanishing points are on the same horizontal line, beyond which you cannot see. This line is the *horizon*.

Viewpoint

The position of the horizon, and of all the vanishing points along it, depends entirely on your viewpoint. By changing your viewpoint you change the position of the horizon, and so alter the perspective.

The 'normal' position of the horizon is at eye level (see diagram A) but, by moving higher up—on to a bridge, for example (diagram B)—you extend your area of vision and the horizon changes. The higher your viewpoint, the higher the horizon.

If you lower your viewpoint, objects appear to grow. A building appears larger because it towers above your normal eye level, indicating that it is very tall in relation to your viewpoint. Conversely, if you get much higher the building appears to become a scaled-down model of itself.

So changing your viewpoint affects the position of the horizon and alters perspective, which, in its turn, governs the

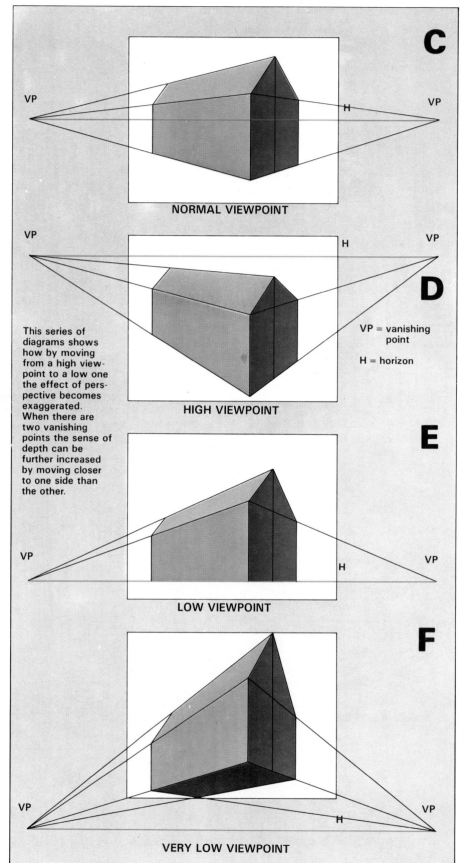

C

NORMAL VIEWPOINT

D

This series of diagrams shows how by moving from a high viewpoint to a low one the effect of perspective becomes exaggerated. When there are two vanishing points the sense of depth can be further increased by moving closer to one side than the other.

VP = vanishing point

H = horizon

HIGH VIEWPOINT

E

LOW VIEWPOINT

F

VERY LOW VIEWPOINT

Two vanishing points are better than one! Especially when it comes to emphasizing the three-dimensional quality of a subject. Take a building, for example—it has two surfaces which meet at right angles to each other so there are two vanishing points, one from each surface. You may not be able to get both, or even one, of these in the shot. But, by positioning yourself in the front of the point where the walls meet, so that both are seen at an angle (above), you can suggest the vanishing points outside the edges of the picture. This will give a greater sense of depth than a shot from head on to just one surface (left).

visual impression of scale. It follows, therefore, that with a very high viewpoint, such as from a helicopter, you could photograph a building as tall as the United Nations Center in New York so that it would assume the scale of a king-size cigarette packet in the resulting print. Your brain, however, would adjust this image, primarily because it would recognize it as being a building, but also because everything else would be in proportion. The building would still stand out and tower above its environment.

Similarly, you could photograph a king-size cigarette packet from a very low viewpoint so that it appeared to tower up like a skyscraper.

Using perspective

Choose a photograph from a newspaper or magazine and draw a carefully measured grid over it. Better still, draw 5mm or 10mm squares on a transparent material or tracing paper. You can then use the grid on any picture without damaging it. With the aid of this grid you will quickly learn how perspective works.

You will be able to see—because your grid has constant, equal squares—how objects steadily appear both narrower and less deep (smaller) as they stretch into the distance. You should also find where the horizon is situated, and thus be able to plot vanishing points.

This will help you notice the way three-dimensional scenes are depicted on the flat surface of a photograph or drawing. Try making better use of perspective as an element of design and composition in your pictures. The next section outlines a number of elements which will help you to create a sense of depth.

Incidentally, if you find yourself able to see the effect of perspective on the print but not through the camera, you might consider, if your camera has interchangeable focusing screens, using one with a squared grid. It may take a little time to get used to it, but you should see a big improvement in your pictures. If you revert to your original screen later, this improvement should remain.

▶ For this picture *Adam Woolfitt* has taken the trouble to find an unusual viewpoint which uses the effect of perspective to its greatest advantage. The flatness of the head-on view against the dynamic lines disappearing into the distance makes a striking contrast, emphasizing both elements.

The essential part that perspective plays in giving a picture a sense of depth and distance is immediately obvious when looking at the print or transparency. It is not so easy to judge through the viewfinder. Placing a grid over printed photographs is one way of getting used to a squared focusing screen, which should help you over the problem. Even if you can't change the focusing screen on your camera you may find that this practice makes you think more carefully before you take your next picture.
Michael Busselle

Patterns

We live surrounded by pattern. In photography these patterns can tease, amuse or stimulate the visual imagination. Skilfully used, this repetition of shapes or lines within a photograph help create a rhythm and order that can make a particular picture memorable. The patterns the photographer uses need not always be exact geometric repetitions like the arches in a colonnade; they could be an impression of a pattern, such as the expanding ripples of water, or tracery of branches against the sky.

Where to find pattern
Finding patterns is very much a question of being aware. To develop your 'eye', look out for pictures with a strong element of pattern and see how they are formed.

Pattern can exist almost everywhere. There are two main types—transient patterns which exist only at a certain moment or from a particular viewpoint, such as the faces of a crowd at a football match, in a flock of flying birds or a parade of soldiers; and static patterns which are man-made or created by nature, such as the windows in an office block or a row of houses, the bark of a tree or the ripples left in sand after the tide has gone out.

How to use pattern
It is unlikely that a picture relying solely on pattern will have any lasting appeal—although it may have an initial impact—so pattern should be used only as a strong element of a picture and not as the sole reason for taking it.

A strong pattern can create a reassuring, restful and ordered atmosphere in a picture. But remember that patterns are usually quite busy and complex, so the main subject of the picture should be simple and bold, and placed in a strong position within the frame, otherwise it may be completely overwhelmed.

▶ **REPETITION**
A far more dynamic effect is created by this diagonal pattern of soldiers than by the usual straight-on rows. The build-up of repeated shapes, repeated angles, repeated details, all contribute to the overall result. The high position is important; at ground level the pattern would not have emerged as clearly. Notice too how the epaulettes separate the rows dramatically.
Bruno Barbey

How light affects pattern

A subject which has an inherent pattern, such as a pile of logs or a row of houses, may not be greatly affected by a change of lighting, but there are other images where the pattern is created or revealed by the nature of the light. A pattern of this sort may only exist for a short time. Take, for example, the patterns caused by sunlight on the ripples of water. It is quite easy to photograph a couple of dozen frames on a subject like this and for each one to be quite different. In many instances it is the shadows which make a pattern, and a slight shift in the angle of light causes the pattern to disappear.

Pattern and colour

Pattern is made up of lines and shapes. In a black and white photograph these are formed by highlights and shadows and contrasting shades of grey. In colour photography, lines and shapes are often formed entirely of colour and

▼ An Italian village, seen at late afternoon when the sun is at an angle. Very strong lighting has created dense shadows and strong highlights, making a pattern which would be equally obvious in black and white.

◄ This reflection of a colourful boat on rippling water makes a transient pattern which will change with the movement of water and the position of the sun.

the colours of the subjects become as important as highlights and shadows. In many instances strong colours make a pattern obvious and it is quite possible for a pattern to be produced by colour alone. The colours in landscapes and woodland scenes often make strong patterns. Close-up photography often reveals beautiful patterns in the colours of flowers and insects, or in the rainbow patterns found in soap bubbles and oily water.

Patterns exist everywhere but the photographer must be prepared to look for them. It is really only a question of 'tuning in' visual awareness to uncover a limitless source of subject matter.

Pattern can be man-made or it can occur naturally. It can be revealed by lighting or colour or by a changed viewpoint. All these pictures contain strong patterns of one sort or another. Some are immediately obvious, such as the repeated shapes of the honeycomb, the sea urchins, the cars seen from above, or the house fronts. Others, such as the umbrellas or the stone wall, depend on the lighting to make the pattern obvious. Often going in close on a detail will show pattern more effectively than photographing the whole—for example, the pattern of leaves (top left) or the fir trees.

Tone and contrast

Tone is the difference in density between the lighter and darker parts of a photograph, ranging from white at the one extreme, to black at the other. In between lies an infinite variety of tones and it is tonal contrast (or the relationship between these tones) which gives three-dimensional form and depth to a picture. The tonal contrast of an image is affected by the lighting of a subject, its colour and its reflective qualities.

In colour, the same principle applies, although technically the darker tones—in the green of a leaf, for example—are called shades, whereas the lighter tones in a picture are called tints.

Tone and form

If a two-dimensional photograph is to imply a third dimension it needs to include the full tonal range with subtle variations. Much of the photographer's skill lies in recognizing these tones and recording them accurately. First, you need to become aware of them in your subject, even in something which is white. A cloud, for example, is very rarely white all over; it is usually a gradation of white and grey and it is these gradations which give the cloud form and depth.

▶ To achieve a full tonal range you need to balance the tonal quality of the subject with lighting, precise exposure and correct contrast in processing and printing.

◀ Most of the tones in this picture are only a slight variation on mid-grey, as the grey scale below shows. This results from soft lighting accentuated by processing and printing. Higher tonal contrast in the picture could have made the overall effect too fussy. *Herbie Yamaguchi*

▶ Difference in tone between background and foreground add to the feeling of distance created here. The limited—but high—contrasting tonal range is the result of lighting conditions—mist and early morning backlighting—which produces the very pale background with the foreground almost in silhouette. *Herbie Yamaguchi*

How light affects tone

If you photograph a white billiard ball (or an egg) and a disc of white card the same size, and light them from the front so that no shadows or highlights are created, there will be no visible difference between them. If you then move the lighting to the side to create shadows, the difference will immediately be obvious. The white ball will develop a full range of tones from white on the lit side through shades of grey to black in the deepest shadow, and so becomes three-dimensional. Light which creates shadows is also creating tone. You can see the relationship between light and the tones and shadows it creates virtually anywhere—from the window light on a fellow passenger's face in a bus or train to the sunlight on the landscape through which you are travelling. A hard (small source) light such as direct sun creates solid tones with clearly defined steps, whereas the soft light of a cloudy day produces gently changing tones and shadows with imperceptible edges.

How tone affects mood

There is a strong connection between the tonal range of a photograph and the mood it conveys. A picture which consists primarily of the darker tones in the range gives a sombre and serious atmosphere whereas a picture with a full range of tones, bright highlights and crisp shadows creates a lively and cheerful impression. A photograph

The two white bottle pictures show how lighting affects tone and how a large tonal range brings out form and distance. The same soft lighting is used for both but front lighting (below) has produced an almost shadowless image, which makes the picture look flat. Half-side lighting (above) gives strong, well-placed shadows, adding form and depth. *Michael Busselle*

125

▲ Low key pictures are usually found, not created. The sombre, serious mood is helped by slight under-exposure. *Michael Busselle*

▼ A high key picture has light tones with little contrast, but there are usually areas of fine, bold detail in a darker tone, almost like a pencil sketch. *Robin Laurance*

made up of lighter tones has a delicate and often romantic quality.

So the tonal quality of your picture should illustrate the mood you want to convey—a dark-toned (low key) picture of children playing on the beach would be as inappropriate as a delicate light-toned (or high key) portrait to show the character of Count Dracula.

Tone and contrast

Contrast is the relationship between the darkest and lightest tones in a picture. A photograph which has a full range of tones with detail in all but the brightest highlight is considered to be of normal contrast. A picture dominated by very light and very dark tones, with little tonal variation between, is described as high contrast. Where there is only a small difference between the brightest and darkest tones you get low contrast image.

Contrast is partly controlled by lighting. A hard directional light such as bright sunlight tends to create a high contrast image while very soft light— a heavily overcast day, for example— creates a low contrast image.

Colour and contrast

Light and dark colours in a subject give it contrast which is independent of that created by lighting. For example, a bride in a pale wedding dress standing against a dark church door is a high contrast subject, whereas the same bride standing against a white wall would be a low contrast subject. You can also control the contrast in your photographs by the way you handle the lighting. Harsh sunlight will emphasize contrast, producing hard shadows and giving extremes of tone. If you want to reduce this contrast, wait until the harsh direct sunlight has become diffused by clouds.

Developing and printing

In black and white photography, and to a lesser extent with some colour films, it is possible to control contrast by varying the development times; the longer the time, the greater the contrast. Conversely, less development means less contrast. The choice of printing papers can also affect the contrast. Taking grade 2 paper as normal, using grades 3 to 5 will give a higher contrast picture and grades 1 to 0 will give a softer result.

To sum up
For a wide range of tones
● Wait for—or create—softer diffused lighting.
● Calculate your exposure carefully: if in doubt, bracket exposures.
● Develop and print according to manufacturers' instructions.

To increase contrast
● Use harsher, direct lighting.
● Under-expose by about 1 stop.
● Increase development and/or use a more contrasty printing paper.

Photographing people

Of all the subjects you are likely to photograph, your fellow human beings have the greatest appeal. Ask any newspaper or magazine what attracts readers, and the reply will be human interest. It's enough just to capture the right smile or a brief glance, even if the subject is unknown to the viewer of the picture.

Many of your pictures of people will, of course, be of friends and family. Often photographers take much more care with pictures of total strangers than they do with family snaps. If you can be a little different, and make really interesting family portraits and candid shots, then people will find the results much more interesting.

Photography is a social activity, and the camera is often a good introduction to others. In other circumstances it can be almost like a weapon, aimed at a target, catching them unawares. In the studio it usually leaves the photographer's hands and eye to stand on a tripod, and becomes much more neutral, so that relaxed formal or informal portraits are readily obtained. At social events, it can provide a record of everyone there for all to enjoy and remember in the future, and there are very few occasions in life where a camera is not welcome.

A posing guide

A photograph of a person freezes a fraction of a second of their life: it shows only a tiny instant of reality, but fixes it forever, in great detail. This is why it is often necessary to pose the subject of your photograph.

When you are with someone, their gestures and movements over a period of time give a *cumulative* impression of the way they look. In a photograph, all this has to be conveyed instantaneously. In addition, when you are with someone you tend to focus attention on one particular part of them—most probably their eyes—and ignore much of the rest. In a photograph you are at leisure to inspect all those forgotten outposts— the awkward position of the legs, or the tightly clenched hands.

A professional model is experienced in maintaining a relaxed appearance for the benefit of the camera. You could ask her to throw her head back and laugh for a pose and she should be able to return to very much the same position for the next shot as well. With inexperienced sitters, though, you should make the pose as straightforward as possible. In this article we deal with solving the problems you might come across with simple, seated poses.

To begin a picture session, first provide a comfortable chair—not too high, or low or with unwieldy arms—and ask your subject to sit quite naturally. Then study the image in the viewfinder and suggest ways to improve it.

Poses for photography are infinitely variable. The secret of being able to tell a good pose from a bad one is to concentrate on the image in the viewfinder *as a picture*—or even as a piece of design. A wide smile that captivates your attention when you take the shot will not make up for the fact that the model's neck looks unnaturally twisted and awkward in the final picture. But remember, this critical scrutiny is your job, not your subject's. Nothing makes an inexperienced subject so nervous as having the various parts of their body shoved around as objects. So let the model feel, move and act as freely as possible and make up your own mind about what is the most suitable pose.

▼ **Dancers and models are trained to move gracefully: they know how to look good. Inexperienced subjects may need the photographer's help.** *Sanders*

▲ Widespread legs—even in trousers—and spread fingers make this pose look rather disjointed.

▲ The knees together slims the pose; linking the hands makes a harmonious circle of the arms.

▼ Folded arms look dull and lack grace and the clearly visible sole of the foot is not very attractive.

▼ By crossing the other leg the sole disappears. The angled arms and hands now add life to the pose.

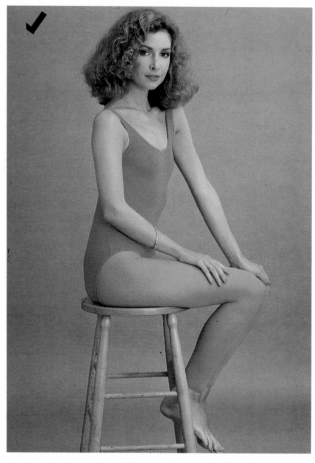

▲ A slouched back makes the subject look rather weary and accentuates the bulge of her stomach.

▲ Straightening up solves all this, and slightly turning the shoulders gives the arms a better line.

▼ Even the shapeliest legs look better if they are in pairs: like this, the subject's slim legs look gawky.

▼ By keeping her knees together at a slight angle, in this shot she shows off her sleek calves.

▲ From the front, the foreshortening makes the subject's thighs and toes look much too big.

▲ Masking the left thigh with her knee and pointing her toes gives the pose a far tidier line.

▲ Though the pose is good, the subject is not relaxed: note that her head is not really resting on her hand.

▲ A word of encouragement can give the subject the confidence to relax into a comfortable position.

With enough time—and enough film—to experiment a little, you can work out a series of movements for your subject and shoot during the action. This can add life and movement to the pictures in the swing of the hair or the flow of the clothes.

Photographing children

Photographing your own children is one of the most rewarding pleasures for the parent with a camera. And with a subject as fascinating as a growing family, you can build up just as memorable a record with a compact, cartridge or instant camera as with an expensive SLR.

Between birth and school age a child can never be left alone: one or other parent is with the child at nearly all times and so the photographic opportunities are many. Playing, bathing, eating, dressing—even sleeping—may not seem the most photogenic of activities, but they are what go to make up each day of childhood. For a true record, the parent should not neglect the moments of frustration, irritation and tears: these emotions are as interesting to look back on as all the fun and laughter.

So always keep a camera handy: it is very easy to say to yourself that you will take some pictures tomorrow, when you are less busy, or after a child's bath when he or she looks at his or her best. And so you miss a shot which might never present itself again. Every day your child gets older—one more day passes, never to be repeated—and before you know it another year has gone by.

Your child and the camera

Children are usually fascinated by cameras, but they are often quite camera-shy. They may curl up, hiding their faces behind arms and hands, and the more coaxing you do, the more shy they become. Bribery is one way to get round the problem, though a simpler solution is to make use of whatever reaction presents itself at that moment: if your child hides his head, photograph what you see. It will have its funny side, then and in the future.

Candid shots often say more than shots taken under posed conditions where it can be difficult to bring out the true nature of the child. While friends may not be able to see this, it is important to remember that you are taking the pictures for yourself, for the rest of the family, and for the children themselves when they grow up.

Techniques

The parent photographer has to be alive to every opportunity for a candid shot. Obviously you can't carry a camera round your neck all the time, but you can keep one handy—not in a drawer or in its case but on the sideboard or the mantelpiece. 'Grab-shots' usually make the best child photographs, but they will only be successful if you are familiar with your camera, so that you can take pictures quickly.

If you do not have an automatic exposure camera, it is a good idea to keep the camera pre-set at the correct exposure for normal lighting conditions in your home. Alternatively keep a small flash gun attached to the camera. If you also pre-set the focusing distance at about 1·5m, you will be able to 'grab' pictures quickly without being delayed by technical problems.

As children tend to have boundless energy and cannot sit still for more than a few seconds, you may have to use a fairly fast shutter speed to stop the action. The aperture will have to be correspondingly large and focusing the more accurate. Using a wide aperture has an advantage, however, in that it throws the background out of focus. This is often very helpful in rooms

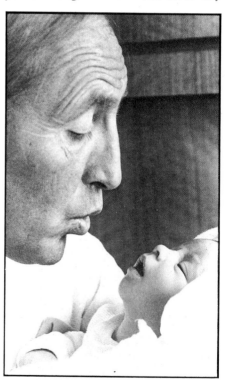

▲ **START ON DAY ONE**
Helmut Gritscher set out to make a complete photographic record of his son Thomas. He enlisted the help of a friend to take this shot of father and son on the first day.

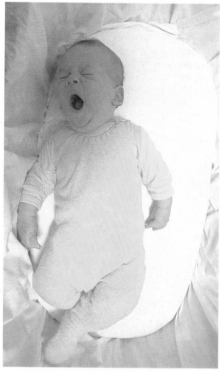

▲ **THOSE FIRST EXPRESSIONS**
With your subject still immobile, what you must hope for is the odd smile or yawn. *Gritscher* shot this from above with a 21mm lens in daylight filtered through the cot and fill–in flash.

▲ **CAPTURING A TODDLER**
At this age your first problem is to catch your subject. With Thomas rooted to his chair and concentrating hard, *Gritscher* homed in with a 90mm lens, lighting the shot with bounced flash.

132

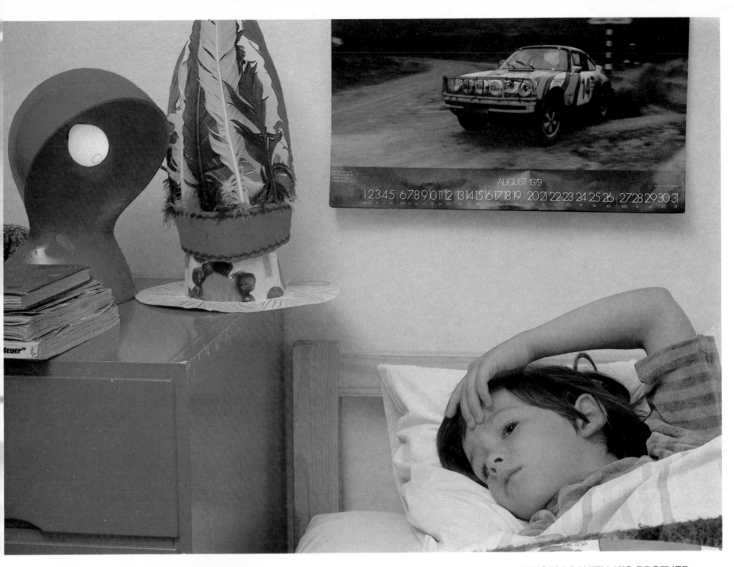

▲ YOUR CHILD'S BEDROOM
By the age of five your child's room already reflects his character, making a telling background. In fact here Thomas is only part of the picture: *Gritscher* composed the shot to show more of his favourite toys than of the boy himself. Bounced flash 'kills' the effect of the bedside lamp.

▼ THOMAS WITH HIS BROTHER
When photographing your children together, wait for the moment which best shows their relationship. Here Thomas, the elder, is absorbed in his game while his younger brother looks on. Fill–in flash supplements the daylight, and the pale tabletop helps to reflect light up into their faces.

▲ ASLEEP IN THE CAR
As toddlers spend much of their lives asleep, use the opportunity to take typical shots. *Gritscher* used a 21mm lens (as Thomas's large feet show) and flash bounced from the car roof.

cluttered with toys and household paraphernalia when there is no time to find a camera angle that puts your subject against a plain background. This also applies out of doors. A garden, for example, will be full of plants and other objects that you may not even notice when you take the shot, but which will inevitably show up on the final print.

One useful technique to remember is to take pictures looking up at or down on your child, which helps to eliminate these unwelcome distracting backgrounds. Carpet, lawns and skies all make excellent foils for your small subject and, in addition, the occasional high viewpoint will reflect the way you normally see him. He will have to look up at you—as he usually has to when you communicate with him.

The right moment

A child's life does not only revolve round his house and garden. There are trips to the shops, journeys by bus, train and car which are seldom regarded as photogenic situations. Cameras tend to be put away as soon as it begins to rain. But what could be more evocative than a picture of a child with his nose pressed to a steamed–up car window and with rain spattering outside? Or a shot of his first ride in a supermarket trolley? There is always a very special quality about 'first time' pictures—the first time your son rode a two–wheeler, caught a fish, rode on an elephant at the zoo—since they are ideal reminders of these occasions.

Even the special occasions which involve careful planning—like birthdays, parties, picnics in the park—can yield unexpected photographs. Surprise is a very positive reaction, and registers very clearly on a child's face. The photographer who can capture real surprise on the face of a child has begun to master the art—and the technicalities—of photographing children.

A photograph which registers some strong emotion in the child has a special poignancy: surprise is one, another is joy. But it is no use manipulating your child's emotions for the benefit of the camera. It will invariably show.

Compiling an album

The family photograph album can be more than just a convenient place to store a random selection of photographs. Instead of sticking the pictures down in the order in which they come back from the processor, you can use the pages to tell a story. For example, a

▲ CLOSE–UP SHOTS
With a long lens, *John Garrett* **peeked under his son Nicholas' hat and into his thoughts. A shot this close needs care in focusing, and the enveloping hat demands careful exposure, with an eye to the colour of reflected light.**

▶ SET–UP SITUATIONS
Although their father set this shot up specially—in the soft shade of a tree and with the cat as a 'prop'—Nicholas and his young brother have by now forgotten the camera. Use a leisurely afternoon to take a series of shots.

series of pictures of one of your children at different ages but doing the same thing—sitting at a desk, perhaps, or riding a rocking horse. Or a group of pictures of different children as they begin to take an interest in the same toys at a particular age, which will illustrate either the similarities or the differences in their approaches to things. One child may have the habit of sucking his finger and another of fiddling with his hair: put these comforting habits together on one page. They are tangible links with the past, a forceful reminder of childhood even when the habit has long been forgotten. Photography can bridge the generation gap, too. Grandchild and grandparent may have 50 years separating them, but look closely at your old family photographs for likenesses and mannerisms that carry through the generations and can be brought out with one click of the shutter.

Family links and likenesses can also be brought out by techniques like multiple exposure or multiple printing from a carefully thought out series of exposures. You can make combination prints from portraits, either linking the features of mother, father and children together or showing the same child at different ages. Similarly, pictures of different children all at the same age can be printed on the same photograph: the result may show likenesses that you could never see when the shots were taken. Without photographs it is all too easy to forget what your children looked like at a certain age.

▶ SPONTANEOUS PICTURES
On the spur of the moment, even the professional photographer can miss his framing. But though here he cuts off his hands and feet, *Garrett* still shows the boy's gleeful mood. A slow shutter speed conveys his quick movements.

Portraits

Informal poses

You will usually get a more natural looking photograph if you choose a comfortable position for your subject. A forced pose will almost inevitably produce a stilted portrait. Always suggest to your subject what to do with his hands. If you leave them to dangle you will not only have an unhappy model who doesn't know what to do, but your pictures will look awkward.

Avoid having your subject facing straight into the lens. Try turning him away slightly and then bringing the head and eyes back into the lens. Or try a profile (though this does accentuate nose and chin, which may be unflattering to some people). Make the eyes the point of focus but, if one eye is markedly nearer the camera, focus on the bridge of the nose.

Photographing people in their own environment helps them to relax and also shows something of their personality. But background detail can be distracting and many photographers prefer to keep backgrounds to a minimum. It is tempting, for example, to turn an outdoor portrait into a landscape, particularly on holiday. Scenery should in fact form a pleasant but not distracting backcloth. Alternatively, you can lose most of the background by using a wide aperture to give you less depth of field. Indoors, keep to a plain wall (or, if you do not have one, cover a patterned wall with a plain sheet) unless you want the background to say something about your subject.

A tripod is not as essential as many photographers believe it to be. You will certainly need one if your chosen exposure requires a speed of less than 1/60. And if used with a cable release, it gives you the freed to move away from the camera and so break that eye-to-eye tension. Otherwise, using a tripod can be a disadvantage because it makes the session more formal and means the photographer cannot change his camera position quickly.

▲ An artist at work. The colours of his clothes are strong enough to stand out from the surroundings, which act as a pleasing backcloth. *James Carmichael*

◀ The strength of this portrait lies in its vivid colours and careful judgement. A 105mm lens at 3m enabled the photographer to go in close. *Spike Powell*

Distortions

The final results of a portrait session are sometimes disappointing. The photograph may be distorted, either because of a technical error such as the lens you use (see pictures below), or because the camera has picked up an unflattering characteristic—an inclination of the head or a blemish of the skin, perhaps—which is barely noticeable until it is put on film. By altering the angle of view, you will be able to play down its prominence. Watch out, too, for rounded shoulders, stray wisps of hair and untidy folds or creases in clothes.

Formal portraits and lens distortion

For a head-and-shoulders portrait, the subject must fill the frame because having to enlarge a small part of a negative to get head and shoulders only will produce a picture of poorer quality. So the photographer has to make sure that the image on the negative is as large as possible. But going in too close can cause distortion of the features.

The answer is to know your lenses and the distortion they produce, so that you can decide which to use in each case.

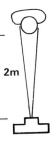

▲ The most practical portrait lens is probably the 135mm. There is no distortion of the features and the photographer does not have to get too close to the subject—an advantage if the sitter is at all self-conscious.

▲ Using a 50mm (standard) lens close enough to the subject to fill the frame produces some distortion on the nose.

▲ Move the 50mm lens back about 2m (roughly 12 times the distance between nose and ear) and there is no distortion, but the face does not fill the frame. You can enlarge a portion of the picture, but the print will be grainy.

▲ If you try to fill the frame with a wide angle lens the features will become distorted. The closer in you go, the more extensive the distortion.

A simple studio

While a studio with its sophisticated lighting equipment offers the ultimate in controlled photographic conditions, it is by no means essential for successful portraiture. Even the most modest living room can be turned into an improvised studio with a few simple adaptations to lighting, background and props.

The natural light through a window is often sufficient, particularly if you use faster film—say 400 ASA, which is available in both colour and black and white. If there is not enough light, however, you can supplement it without using more advanced lighting which is fully discussed in later chapters.

One way of providing extra light indoors is to use flash, either pointed directly at the subject or bounced off a light-coloured ceiling or wall. Bounce flash gives a more even distribution of light, handy if you want to include something of the background, while direct flash focuses attention on the subject himself. The problem with flash, however, is that you cannot see the effect it is creating before you release the shutter.

The more satisfactory answer is to substitute photoflood bulbs for normal bulbs in standard or table lamps. These are available from 275 watts upwards and, as a guide, a room about 5m

square with light-coloured walls and ceiling and one large window may need only one 275-watt bulb. These bulbs get very hot, so remove lampshades before switching on. And, if you are taking colour slides, use tungsten balanced film.

Curtains at the window can be used to create an effective background by draping them behind the subject and

fastening them against the wall. If your curtains or background wall are patterned, however, use a plain sheet which is less distracting.

Start by giving your subject a simple household chair. He can sit on it, lean on it, rest a foot on it or sit back to front on it. A Victorian armchair lends itself to a formal portrait while a kitchen chair creates a casual look.

▲ For an atmospheric portrait the photographer used a black stocking over the lens, and 400 ASA film for graininess.

◄ Because she was comfortably seated, the subject was able to stay quite still while the photographer took this photograph using a tripod and slow exposure.

▶ To use his living room as a studio, the photographer tied one curtain back to let in maximum light and positioned his subject close to the window. Because it was a dull day he had to use a slow exposure and a tripod. A helper held a piece of white board to reflect light and no other source of light was used. For some pictures a black stocking stretched tightly over the lens and held with a rubber band helped to diffuse the light.

▶ Far right: by positioning his subject so that light from the window was reflected back to her shadow side, the photographer was able to use a slow film to give him a good quality print.

138

Photographing and arranging groups

For many photographers, the invitation to any social event—a wedding, a christening, even a family outing—may be accompanied by the request: 'And, please, bring your camera.' The advantage of photographing people who are all fully aware of the camera is that you can expect their co-operation: the problem is that you can't always depend on it. With planned groups, self-consciousness is your chief enemy. By the time you have the group you want, you may find that those cheerful faces have turned to stone and the results are far from the friendly gathering you set out to portray.

The successful planned group photograph shows every member to advantage yet forms a pleasing arrangement when viewed as a whole. Your chief difficulty will be in remembering the composition while dealing tactfully with the personalities involved. Plan as much as possible in advance. If your subject is a sports team, for example, think out your colour scheme beforehand, working out what background to use. Or, if the group includes children and adults, plan how to deal with their varying heights. Planning can save time—and tempers too—on the day. If you can arrange the group quickly, the results are less likely to show tell-tale signs of boredom and restlessness. When the session begins, establish your authority right away, at the same time persuading your subjects to participate—to think about what you are trying to do. Identify everybody by name, and use their names when giving your directions. Make these directions clear and to the point: you will lose their attention if you are indecisive.

Lighting

The ideal lighting for groups is bright but even. Check before you start shooting that each face is similarly lit. In direct sunlight you may find the shadow of one member of a group falling across the person next to him. And there is sure to be someone who

▼ At a royal wedding the photographer has little control over the situation. Wherever possible, keep bright colours to the middle and look for details to break a monotonous line. *Howell Conant*

▲ An Edwardian family posed against a painted backdrop: (right) alternating black and white areas are balanced and the babies' legs are arranged to lead the eye towards the centre.

can't help squinting all the time. But the light does need to be bright so that you can shoot with a small aperture to maintain a large depth of field and good definition throughout the picture.

Arranging the group

How do you go about arranging a group in anything but a straight line? Consider a group of three to start with. You only have to turn the two outer figures slightly towards the centre, and you already have an improvement on a straight line-up. Try to decide before-hand what your subjects should do with their hands, and make that one of your first directions. This will not only improve the final picture but will also help the group to relax: people who are self-conscious in front of a camera find this one of the most agonizing pro-blems. If you are moving in close—shooting from the waist up—it is best to keep it fairly uniform with arms folded or hands clasped in front as a sort of frame for the bottom of your picture. If you have got more space, try varying the positions more—one person with arms folded, one with hands in pockets or behind his back.

◄ Here the three bright heads, all against dark backgrounds, form a central pattern. Below them, white chair legs slope in to contain the group. *Richard Greenhill*

▼ Planned groups need not be formal. The position of the three faces on the right and the leaning figures are carefully composed, yet seem relaxed. *Clay Perry*

Props and location

You can tell the viewer a great deal about any group of people simply by adding props or choosing an appropriate location. The most obvious 'prop' of course is a uniform. A group of solicitors might each be holding a bundle of papers tied with that telltale ribbon; the local fishing club would have rods and nets.

Try varying the direction in which you get your subjects to look. Include one shot with them all looking into the camera but experiment with their eyes looking just above and either side of the camera. And don't always insist on a smile: in the wrong situation smiles can look very forced and unnatural.

Composition will be a lot easier if there is something to form the group around. Take a single arm-chair, for example, and that same group of three. With the chair at an angle of about 45° to the camera, ask one to stand at the back, the second to sit and the third to perch on the arm of the chair. They turn their heads to the camera, but the angles of their bodies

▲ As these children are perched on a wall, a straight line-up is unavoidable: lively colour emphasizes their mood. *Richard Greenhill*

▶ Backlighting makes this group stand out from its surroundings and also helps with detail by reducing contrast on the faces.

give the group cohesion.

The same principles apply when you add two or three more to a group. You may need two chairs or a sofa; outside you could use a bench, a fallen tree trunk or a flight of steps. But vary the heights as before, and have the outer members of the group turned inwards slightly towards the centre. You can add to the informality of the picture by getting some members of the group to look into the group while others look towards the camera. If there are children in the group, a book or a toy on their knees will keep them occupied between shots and add to the picture's relaxed atmosphere.

◄ Photographing Generation X in his studio on Ektachrome 64, *Gered Mankowitz* used backlighting and low frontlighting to cast menacing shadows on their faces.

▼ What begins as a candid shot may be improved if the subjects become aware of the camera and will co-operate. You need not ask them to pose: shift your own position to get the best grouping. *John Bulmer*

Photographing girls

Photographing girls is a huge part of the business of professional photography, and a complete industry has evolved to provide models for photographers and art directors. Every major city has a network of model agencies whose files contain a face and figure for every occasion, and the selection of the right model has become a responsible and demanding job. The girl on all the posters—sipping an aperitif, or eating chocolates—may well have been one of fifty interviewed, many of whom will have been called back for a test session.

For the enthusiast who simply wants to take pictures of an attractive girl, this complicated selection process will seem quite unnecessary. He has only himself to please, not the public at large. Nevertheless the right choice of model determines the success of the session for the amateur as much as for the professional, and a little objective thought beforehand can save a lot of disappointment later. If you belong to a camera club, you may find that studio glamour sessions are periodically organized for the members, and for your first attempt at this type of photography it may be advisable to take advantage of the studio and the professional model they choose. Alternatively you may prefer to choose your own model and organize the setting.

Choosing your model

First of all, you should only ask a girl whom *you* find attractive. This may seem obvious but it is easy to be misled by helpful friends who 'know someone who knows someone who would make a wonderful model.' Whoever you find attractive is your best model. It is not necessary to change your tastes for a photograph: the media condition us to believe that only tall, young, slim

blondes are suitable models, even though we may find buxom brunettes more attractive.

For the first few sessions it is wise to choose someone you know fairly well and can be at ease with. Being relaxed is most important for both photographer and model, and though this comes mainly with experience, the beginner can do a great deal to eliminate unnecessary awkwardness.

Clothes and make-up

Your choice of clothes for the model should take account of the mood of the pictures you want to take as well as the model's own preference. Do not encourage her to dress up (or down) in a way which is alien to her. She should feel as natural as possible, since self-

consciousness is the most destructive element in this type of picture. Ask her to bring a selection of clothes (a choice of colours is also important when shooting in colour) because often the background and lighting will influence what she wears. It can also be handy to have a small selection of accessories as props—scarves, jewellery or even a hat—which can sometimes add the touch that completes the picture.

Make-up is rather more difficult. It can often contribute to the success of a picture but it can, if used indiscreetly, be a disaster. Too little rather than too much is the best general rule. Slightly tinted powder is useful to kill unwanted shine on the skin, a little mascara adds definition to eye lashes, and a darker shade of lipstick can often

1 Flirtatious
For these studio shots, *Martin Riedl* used a simple lighting set-up—one diffused side-light and a reflector—using a wind machine to give more life to his model's hair.

2 Picture making
Outdoors, choose locations that contribute to your pictures: framing her in a window gives extra realism to this girl's pose.

◀ One way of finding a model for glamour photography is to join in a camera club session—either in a studio or on location. Though you may forfeit complete control of the model, you will gain valuable practice at working with a professional model at a fraction of the cost.

3 Natural

The summer countryside is an ideal background, and less daunting than a studio for an inexperienced model. If possible, choose a hazy day for softer lighting effects. *Michael Busselle* opened up to f2·8 to allow the flowers in front and behind to drop out of focus.

4 Story telling

With a careful choice of props, clothes and background, you can make your pictures tell a story. Here the realistic effect created in the studio is reinforced by natural-looking lighting —electronic flash through a very large diffuser and boosted by a reflector.

5 Humourous

Incongruous settings and props can give your pictures a bizarre humour. Tricky lighting on this beach gave a reading of 1/250 at f8.

add shape to the mouth—particularly in a full length shot, or when shooting in black and white.

Using make-up to shade the face—such as blusher on the cheek bones—is best avoided unless applied expertly and under controlled lighting conditions. Make-up is discussed more fully in a later section. Make-up can mask any obvious skin blemishes, and when a lot of bare skin is going to be visible it usually looks best if it is brown rather than stark white. There are some rather elaborate tanning products, but a tinted sun oil has a similar effect.

Where to shoot

Your setting may be indoors or outdoors, in natural or artificial light, in a studio or on location. If you are a novice you should make the atmosphere of the location as relaxed as possible. It is usually best, particularly if your model is inexperienced too, to avoid the studio set-up with artificial lighting, because so much effort is needed to make it look natural. Even experienced models and photographers can find this quite daunting.

If, on the other hand, you are happiest when you have complete control over lighting and backgrounds, and are more interested in producing studio pictures, this may suit you best.

Whatever situation you choose, make sure you are organized and can give the impression that you know what you are about. Have your camera loaded, meter set to the right ASA, lighting set up in approximate positions, background in position, and any props you might need, such as a chair or a stool, ready and waiting. If it is your first session it's even worth having a rehearsal with someone other than your model, so that when she arrives *you* are relaxed and in charge of the situation. If you choose a more natural setting—using daylight indoors or outdoors—it is equally important to know exactly where to go and to have a good idea of what you are going to do. If you are shooting outdoors you should know where the sun is going to be at the appointed hour. Will you need a reflector to lighten up the shadows, or maybe fill-in flash? Is there somewhere for your model to change and do her make-up? Would some props be useful —a hammock maybe, or a beach chair? If it is going to be a long session, how about a flask of coffee or some cans of cold beer? The more organized you are, the more you will both enjoy the session.

6 Tricks

This picture was shot to be used on its side, cropped to exclude the towel, so that the profile and streaming hair look like a bizarre figurehead. *Tino Tedaldi* used flash close to the lens and exposed six times, each at peak action as the girl flung back her head.

7 Fantasy

Photographing in an old music hall, *James Wedge* used a Contax camera with an 85mm lens and flash directed at the floor for the low, theatrical lighting effect of this picture. He used Ilford FP4 film and hand-coloured the resulting black and white print.

8 Fashion cover

Two sheets of cartridge paper make up this vivid background, the join hidden by the pole. *Howard Kingsnorth* lit the shot with a ring flash around the 150mm lens of his Hasselblad, set at 1/60 and f11.

9 Glamour Girl

Here a graduated filter, normally used to reduce contrast between sky and subject, dramatically darkens the sky. A wide angle lens isolates the model still further by exaggerating the distance to the horizon.

Equipment

All the equipment you use should be familiar to you. Never try out anything new on your first session with a model; it creates a bad impression if you do not seem to know your equipment and it will destroy your confidence if you fumble. A tripod is very useful in this type of photography as the camera can be positioned and left whilst you adjust lighting, take exposure readings and so on. A large reflector, made of card or polystyrene, and something to prop it against are also invaluable, particularly for daylight shots. If you have a camera with interchangeable lenses, a longer lens can be an asset—an 85mm or 105mm on a 35mm camera—as it enables you to work at a distance from your model rather than crowding her. A longer lens can also improve perspective, particularly when you are shooting close-up portraits, and on location it will help you to subdue any problematical background details by throwing them out of focus.

Directing a model

The best rule about directing a model is —don't. The secret is to establish a situation—by your choice of background, props and clothes—in which the model can forget the camera and be herself. Picture-taking should become almost incidental. If, after the first few shots, you are still having to give precise directions—'move your arm to the right, bend your head, turn your eyes to the left'—then something is wrong and it would be better to stop and start afresh. Organised poses can often look false. The real technique of directing a model is to establish an easy rapport, so that she does what is needed of her own accord. This rapport comes from her confidence in you as a photographer, and the efficiency with which you have organized the session. It also comes from the knowledge that you find her attractive, and the fact that you are both enjoying the session. This is true of professional models too: it is very easy to take bad pictures of top models if you lose their confidence and they begin to feel insecure and even unattractive. The often caricatured patter of the fashion photographer—'super, super...oh, *really* nice'—is not as meaningless as it may sound. It is a way of keeping up the constant communication that is vital between the photographer and his model.

Photographing weddings

For the amateur photographer, an invitation to a wedding is a perfect opportunity to practise taking pictures of people. There are the candid shots of anxious faces before the event; the ceremonial views of the procession; formal portraits of bride and groom, family and guests all looking their best; and group pictures which become more and more informal as festivities continue. And what better wedding present for the bride and groom to supplement the professional's pictures.

For many couples, their wedding is the occasion of a lifetime, so an amateur should never attempt to take the official photographic record unless he is absolutely certain that he can cope with ease and that his pictures will come out well. However strongly the couple may try to persuade you, resist them unless you are completely confident of your results: it is always better to play safe for such an unrepeatable occasion, and employ a professional photographer—at least for the wedding ceremony itself. Relieved of the full responsibility, you can take along your camera and go for the less formal shots he may not have time for, or the pictures that may only happen amongst family and friends. But never get in the way of the professional: you may ruin both his and your own photographs and the bride will not thank you for that.

While it is sensible to keep your camera handy at all times, ready for the unexpected opportunity, there are particular moments during the ceremony and the reception that lend themselves to specific types of photography.

Bride at home

Before the bride leaves for the church ask her to give you 10 minutes for informal portraits and full-length shots at home or in the garden. The backgrounds will be far more personal than at the church or hall. She might also have her bridesmaids with her and be able to pose with father, mother and other relations. Only attempt this if you are already quick and efficient at handling your camera and flash. There will not be time for endless meter readings and fumbling.

In the church

As a guest you will probably go into the church before the bride arrives. Try to station yourself on the centre aisle, near the back. Strictly, you should ask the vicar's permission to take pictures in the church but most vicars do not mind a discreet picture taken from the back, without flash and during a hymn, to cover the noise of the shutter. With fast colour film, it is usually possible to get good results at about 1/30 at f2 on a dull day in a dark church, and up to about 1/30 at f5·6 in a bright church. If the ceremony is taking place in a registry office, you will probably be unable to use your camera unless the official photographer has posed some shots and allows you to photograph his set-ups.

After the ceremony

The professional photographer will usually set up and shoot his groups at or near the church door. For the amateur it is best to slip out of the church while the couple are signing the register. Place yourself well to one side of the professional and shoot the groups he arranges at an angle. While he is working, you can turn your lens on to the guests coming out of the church and be watching the proceedings. This will give you some ready-made, informal groups of the guests, close together and all looking the same way. When there is a long path to the cars, take the opportunity for some action shots using a fast shutter speed.

◀ **Before a wedding, the photographer must remain in the background, quietly on the look-out for candid shots of the hectic preparations.** *Derek Bayes* **chose light from a low window rather than obtrusive flash, exposing for 1/60 at f2·8.**

At the reception

Get back to the reception quickly to be first in and to avoid the queue. Keep an eye open for good candid pictures of the couple receiving their guests, but this period can also be used to take the bridesmaids and pages aside (photograph brothers and sisters together, even if one is not an attendant) and find a plain background indoors or a green hedge or bush outdoors to shoot some semi-posed full-lengths and close-ups. Next, try to organize some more candid pictures of the younger ones eating, playing hide-and-seek round a tree, or just holding hands. On sunny days, shoot into the sun, taking a reading on the shadow side, and always use a lens hood. Only use flash fill-in if absolutely necessary when the contrast is very high. Set an automatic flash gun for a film twice as fast as the one you are using. There is usually a pause after the couple have received their guests and before the meal or main reception. This is the time to ask the bride to pose for a few special pictures, with and (if you have not previously taken pictures at her home) without her husband.

You should have chosen your locations, whether in or out of doors, and already worked out the ideas and poses you are going to try and the exposures and equipment you want to use so that you can lead them straight to the spot and start shooting without wasting time. Try for some romantic shots—kissing, touching champagne glasses, looking at the bouquet, or at each other, profiles in semi-silhouette. You will get maximum co-operation if you are quick and efficient.

Cake cutting and speeches

If the professional is to cover the reception he will probably have done a mock cake cutting as soon as the couple returned from the ceremony, so the way will be clear for you when it actually takes place. You might be able to ask the toastmaster or best man to pose them for a picture holding the knife and looking at you before they actually cut the cake when their faces may be hidden. Speech makers are worth a few pictures, and keep an eye open for the reactions of the couple to the traditionally suggestive remarks of the proposer or the best man. During the speeches, position yourself behind and to one side of the couple and try to photograph as many of the guests as you can. You might find it useful to change to a wide angle lens for this. If

▶ Flash-on-camera gives a bland, overall light which flattens detail especially on white dresses and on cakes. Either hold the flash away from the camera or bounce it from a reflecting surface. Here the photographer used electronic flash bounced from an umbrella.

▼ Look for original shots to liven up conventional wedding pictures. *Michael Boys* blocked reflections from outside with his own shadow for a clear view of the bridesmaid.

▲ Reception shots become more candid as guests relax. For a bride's eye view, *John Sims* used a long lens to fill the frame with faces.

▼ As hilarity takes over, be ready for the unexpected. *Archie Miles* set his shutter at 1/250 and released it with the groom in mid-air.

you cannot get enough in from eye level, try holding the camera and flash above your head and pointing it down slightly. This will give you many more faces at the back.

The going-away
This is a great time for candid pictures: the run down the line of guests, confetti, rice, kisses all round, the decorated car, the kiss in the back seat, throwing the bouquet, tears, and everybody waving goodbye. The professional rarely waits for it so make sure you are there.

Camera and equipment
It is essential to have a camera which you know how to use quickly and efficiently. Never buy a new camera to shoot pictures at a special event without taking several experimental reels of film and seeing the results first. It is also fatal to borrow someone else's camera for this sort of occasion.

Medium speed colour negative film is the best all-round film (100-200 ASA). 400 or 1000 ASA film is very useful for low light shots in a church or out of doors on a dark or rainy day, but it is too contrasty to use in bright

sunlight. It is also useful with an accurate electronic flash for far-away groups indoors and out.

You should always buy the best flash gun you can afford: automatic exposure models with a thyristor for quick recycling times are the best. They should be fitted on a bracket to the side of the camera rather than in the hot shoe. This helps to avoid the 'red eye' effect and gives slightly better modelling to faces. Many flash guns can be attached to the camera with an extra 1-metre extension, so the head can be held away from the camera to drop the shadow behind the subject and give even better lighting—but this technique needs lots of practice to avoid the flash pointing one way and the camera another!

Along with equipment, the photographer needs a fair amount of experience and technique to cover a wedding thoroughly. He will also need to expose a lot of film but, for an important family event, that is money well spent. You will probably want to give a set of pictures to the couple as a present, but don't be afraid to charge others a fair price per print to offset your heavy expenses and your time.

Outdoor Photography

Photography can make you aware of the world around you. It is one thing to look at a magnificent view and say 'That's breathtaking' and another to view it through your lens, compose the shot, and take it home with you. In the outdoor world you will at first recognise the dramatic and obvious subject matter in tourist locations, and eventually come to see beauty in unexpected corners. A walk through the wood or down the street can be turned into a journey of visual exploration when you carry an SLR with you.

Holiday time is photography time, with good reason, and you can take much more interesting holiday shots with a little thought beforehand. Your own back garden can also be a source of varied subject-matter. So can the everyday outdoor events you probably attend as a spectator—the camera gets you involved in a new way.

Outdoors, you see the scene change during the day and through the seasons. Dusk and night-time offer different opportunities and show the familiar world as your eyes never see it, because the camera can record the scene faithfully or emphasis mood. With a camera you realise that the world is constantly changing and each day brings fresh subjects in a fresh light.

Landscape photography

Ever since the earliest days of photography, landscapes have been a popular choice of subject. The reasons for photographing landscapes range from the simple desire to record somewhere visited on holiday to the powerful evocation of place and atmosphere evident in photographs like Bill Brandt's pictures of Yorkshire.

Yet for every successful record of a landscape most photographers take many pictures that just don't work out. This is often because what the camera can record in the confines of a rectangular frame seldom matches what the eye can see. On film the most stunning panoramic view tends to look flat and uninteresting and the grandeur of a tall mountain fades to a tiny speck.

Be selective

Part of the thrill of the landscape is to do with being there. What the landscape photographer has to do is find some section, some detail even, that can communicate this thrill to other people. Try the old painters' trick with your hands —make two right angles with your thumbs and first fingers and turn them into a rectangle. Through one half-open eye look at a landscape through the rectangle, varying the distance from your eye, and see how many completely different possibilities are available from one viewpoint.

Move the camera

There are two basic ways to vary the way you record a landscape. The

most important one is to move your-self and the camera until you find the best viewpoint. If, from the road, you see a landscape that cries out to be photographed, take some time ex-ploring the location on foot. Just walking up a slope will frequently open up new viewpoints and can alter dramatically what is seen through the viewfinder. And always look out for details in the landscape—a wall, a clump of trees or a distant building that will give some point to recording that

particular overall view. Often it is a question of building the shapes that make up a landscape into a photograph you will want to look at again and again.

Time of day

To catch a scene at its very best, be pre-pared to come back time after time A certain view seen at sunset may look very different from the way it looked in the middle of the day: not only does the direction of the light change, but the

shadows and the colour of the light do, too. What appears a flat and feature-less landscape at midday may look completely different early in the morn-ing. When the time and the weather are both right then take a great many pic-tures. Some famous photographers of landscapes have earned a high reputa-tion by following this procedure. The sun shines no more for them than others, nor do clouds come in the right places to please them, but when conditions are correct they take maximum advantage.

◄ The force of *Georg Gerster's* picture is in its composition. The ridges form a classic Z, from bottom right to the tree on the left, veering up towards the far trees, then into the blue beyond.

Changing lenses can move mountains. ▲ With a 50mm lens *Peter Goodliffe* keeps his background at a distance. ▼ An 85mm lens brings it closer, helped by a low angle which loses the lake, and the scene narrows.

Weather

Similarly, watch out for sudden changes in the weather which can dramatically alter the appearance of a certain stretch of countryside. For instance, in the Lake District dramatic changes can happen within half an hour during spring or autumn, and in the Mediterranean a storm can quickly transform an unremarkable landscape into an unforgettable one.

And don't be put off by the problems of taking photographs in bad weather, as it is precisely these unexpected changes in light and visibility that can change the expected holiday view into something special.

There are certain practical things that the photographer can do to make use of these changes or to overcome the problems they create. Filters can be a great help here. In colour, a U/V filter reduces some of the problems of photographing through mist or haze. A polarizing filter helps to darken a blue sky. In black and white a yellow or orange filter accentuates cloud formations against a blue sky. A medium or deep red filter further increases the contrast between a landscape and a blue sky, producing an aggressive, dramatic image.

In certain light, distant views often look mauvy-blue. This is called 'aerial perspective' and painters often use the trick of emphasizing the blue haze to create the effect of distance. Photographers can do the same by using a pale blue filter to accentuate the misty quality of the light.

The biggest single source of disappointment in landscape results is the final size of the image. If the subject is too distant, the result on the print will be too small. The general panoramic shot is rarely successful unless some detail has been selected from it. The question of image size can be solved in one of two ways: either use a lens of longer focal length to select part of the panorama or, if you have only a standard 50mm lens or a fixed lens camera, move the camera closer to a detail.

What camera for landscapes

You can use any format of camera for landscape photography. Here the problem of size and portability is simply a question of convenience; the more cumbersome, large format cameras will give fine quality results, although slow 35mm films in both colour and black and white are capable of very acceptable image quality. It is the possibility of changing to another lens—with a different angle of view—that makes the 35mm SLR the camera used by most keen amateur landscape photographers. The telephoto lens (from about 105mm to 200mm) will allow the photographer to enlarge distant detail, making the background look imposing in relation to mid-distance objects. This helps overcome one of the main disappointments for photographers with fixed lens cameras when the view that looked spectacular ends up as insignificant in the final print. This ability of the telephoto lens to bring distant detail nearer makes it one of the most useful extra accessories for landscape work.

▲ Distance—and perspective— lend enchantment to this wood. Here *Peter Goodliffe* uses a 28mm lens to exaggerate the height of the trees: the parallel lines rush away from the viewer, converging far more quickly than if they had been shot with a standard or telephoto lens. The wide angle lens also makes it easier to maintain focus throughout, and this, along with a sunburst placed high on the picture, adds to the towering effect. But beware: the results of photographing into the sun, even filtered by foliage, can lead to excessive flare.

▶ Using a wide angle lens at f11 *Bill Colman* keeps sharp focus throughout, from the bright flowers in the foreground to the contrasting scene beyond.

◀ *Barry Lewis* makes spectacular use of colour to show bizarre weather conditions. Using a telephoto lens (1/250 at f5·6), he balances the sunlit yellow fields with the stormy dark sky by positioning the horizon across the centre of the frame.

Wide angle lens

But the other extreme of focal length —the wide angle (28mm or 35mm)—is equally useful in this type of photography. It does the opposite of the telephoto lens—exaggerating the scale of near and mid-distance objects relative to background. For example, it will allow you to work close to a deep valley in order to emphasize its depth and exaggerate the distance to the far horizon.

Provided you can fill the viewfinder, trees look taller and a valley will look deeper than with a normal lens. But it is easy to end up with an even smaller image with this type of lens because of the wider angle of view so make even greater use of foreground elements.

Foreground

Foreground is of great importance in landscape composition, because it helps get over the problem of scale and depth. For example, if you can place a tree, a rock or a person in the foreground, you give an idea of the scale of your subject. Even if the foreground is out of focus it can act as a reference point from which to start looking at the picture.

Exposure problems

The other technical problem the landscape photographer must consider is exposure calculation. It is not as simple as, say, measuring the exposure for a single object 3m from the camera and lit by a single table lamp. With a landscape the light may be reaching the subject in a number of ways; direct sunlight, diffused by clouds, or as reflected light bouncing off water, sand or light-coloured buildings. The subject itself may cover a very large area and parts of it may vary widely in contrast—for example, the difference between a bright sky and a darker area of the landscape, probably in shadow.

In this situation, the safest method is to take an average of the meter readings from the two areas, sky or land, then decide whether one or other is more important to the effect of the picture. If your camera has a TTL (through the lens) meter, tilt the camera up and then down to make the two readings—fill the picture area first with sky, then only land. If you consider that both areas are equally important, set your exposure for midway between the two. One way to make sure of a satisfactory result is to bracket the exposures on either side of the meter reading—a slightly under-exposed foreground may give a more dramatic picture anyway.

Photographing landscapes is not like taking portraits. Landscape features are fixed. You cannot just move hills or trees around to improve your pictures. You must move the camera and choose the best lens to suit the photograph.

And yet, to produce striking landscape pictures, the same sort of compositional rules must be followed. That is, there must be a balance between the light and dark areas of the frame, the colours must work together, the design should be clear and direct—and so on. There-fore you have to select with care just what you want to be included in your picture. You must also decide on the degree of emphasis you wish to give each component of the picture—in other words, ask yourself *why* you are taking it. And finally, you must try to exclude any ugly or irrelevant details from the shot. The only ways you can control these many different elements are–

1) careful choice of camera viewpoint (that is, where you decide to stand to take the picture);

2) choice of lens, which governs the 'angle of view';

3) careful framing of the subject, so that the picture includes all you want but excludes, or hides, unwanted details.

Unwanted details

Landscapes, however beautiful, are often spoiled by that over-flowing waste paper basket in the foreground. Tele-graph poles, electricity pylons and other man-made objects can also spoil a natural scene. Sometimes a slight change

of camera position can place these either at the edge of the picture, or out of frame completely. By moving a few paces backwards or forwards you may be able to hide a pylon behind a tree. Quite a small tree in the foreground of a picture can hide much larger objects that are in the distance.

Trees, fences and other objects can also be used to direct the eye to the main interest of a distant landscape. They can act as a 'frame' and produce a strong composition, too.

An alternative is sometimes to use a longer focal-length lens. For example, change from a wide-angle or standard to a short telephoto (85 to 135mm). Instead of photographing the wide sweep of a landscape, be more selective. Isolate the main point of interest, while still excluding the telegraph poles or the pylons.

Brightness and colour

When looking at a picture, the eye is drawn most strongly to bright areas and brightly coloured objects. Any strong colour will attract the viewer's attention. These factors affect the whole balance of a composition. If the bright area or bright colour is the main attraction of a picture, then of course this is not a problem. However, landscape colours—being natural—are often fairly muted. Browns, greens and blues are the most common colours. Any bright colours are likely to be unnatural—for example, a brightly coloured car, which is reflec-

◀ **The land dominates this shot by *Jean Bichet*, with a high horizon delicately indicated by the line of trees. The eye is drawn into the picture down the furrows which lead to the dominant colour of the yellow field.**

▼ **Taken in Idaho, USA. *Sergio Dorantes* lay flat on his belly to achieve the low horizon in this shot. To emphasize the cloud detail and improve colour saturation, he used a polarizing filter on an 80mm lens. Exposure was 1/30 at f11 on Kodachrome 25.**

ting the sunlight. This may produce such a strong effect that it overpowers the interest of the natural landscape you are trying to capture.

Again, try to choose a viewpoint, lens and framing which produce the effect you want.

Every picture has a purpose, even if it is simply to record a beautiful scene. This purpose must always dominate your thinking. Successful landscape pictures are produced only when you *consciously* consider everything in the viewfinder in detail, and not just the overall effect. Observation of detail is what makes an excellent landscape photographer.

Placing the horizon

Almost every landscape picture will have a horizon. The placing of this horizon can make a considerable difference to the success or failure of the picture. Usually the horizon is placed according to the 'rule of thirds'—that is, it is placed one third from the top or one third from the bottom of the picture. This technique almost invariably produces a balanced-looking picture. Where *exactly* to place the horizon depends on the relative 'weights' of the land mass and the sky. If the sky is very light or plain, it will carry less interest than the landscape itself. Therefore if you include too much sky in the picture the balance will be wrong. A heavier sky (that is one with an interesting group of clouds, perhaps) can be used to good effect to take up a larger area of the picture.

If you are using a tree or some other

dark object as a frame, to provide a lead-in to the picture, this will increase the weight of the picture above the horizon. This allows you to place the horizon lower down while still keeping the overall balance right.

The horizon can also be placed very close to the top or bottom of the picture. This can produce a very dramatic effect, with the right subject. With the horizon at the bottom of the picture, the result is a cloudscape rather than a landscape. This can give a light and airy effect. With the horizon at the top of the frame, the result can be rather heavy unless the landscape itself is varied enough. The 'rule of thirds' is a good general guide to placing the horizon, but like all the 'rules' of composition, it can be broken if you wish.

Symmetry and balance

Putting the horizon in the middle of the picture seldom works. Similarly, if there is no horizon, placing the main interest of a scene in the centre of a landscape picture seldom works. Pictures like this may be symmetrical, but symmetry is not the same as balance. However, the 'rule of thirds' can be used again. If you divide each side of the picture into thirds, there are four points where these thirds intersect. Placing the main interest on one of these points—that is one third from the side of the frame—generally produces a

balanced picture, which is again satisfying to look at.

Again, the rule can be broken. It is possible for a perfectly symmetrical picture (such as a reflection picture) to be very effective. But such pictures are the exception rather than the rule. Remember in all cases that it is the total combination of all the elements in the frame that dictate the balance of a composition, and dictate whether the picture is a success or not.

Camera angle and position

When considering balance, consider also the way in which you hold and point the camera. Many otherwise excellent landscapes have been ruined by the photographer not noticing that the camera was tilted slightly to one side. This produces a horizon which is not level. If the picture includes a lake, loch or sea, this can give the unfortunate impression that the sea is running downhill!

Remember also that there are many good camera positions apart from the usual, eye-level view. You can sometimes improve a landscape picture by finding a higher viewpoint—even if this is only by standing on a wall. You can also lower the camera to ground level. This gives a feeling of greater involvement with the subject. You can also use any plants and flowers as part of a frame, or to hide unwanted detail. This

▶ This landscape has five elements blending together; the foreground tree (provides scale), the trees in shadow and those in sunlight, the rocks and sky. *G. Marshall Smith* chose a good moment to press the shutter, the lighting and colours lead your eye into the picture, among the trees and up to the rocks.

▲ *Colin Molyneux* took this picture late on a March evening in South Wales. He was on the opposite side of the valley with the camera and a 400mm lens on a tripod. The components of the picture balance each other well; the bushes (left) balance the field (right), and the sun adds interest to a plain sky.

technique can be particularly useful with a wide-angle lens.

Shape

The standard sizes of slides and prints need not limit the shape of your pictures. To be effective, a landscape picture sometimes needs to be square, or an unusual shape—such as very long but narrow. Some firms make non-standard slide mounts you can use to produce unusual picture shapes. Also, you can trim printing papers to suit the shape of the landscape. But for successful pictures of this sort, it is best to consider the final shape *before* you take the picture in the first place.

Holiday photography

A camera has become as essential a part of holiday equipment as suntan oil and paperbacks. Everyone wants to come back with a record of it all on film. But the danger is that the holiday-maker tends to press the button frantically at whatever comes along with no thought for the best way to capture the scene.

Yet holidays are the ideal time to plan pictures. Away from normal daily routine, the photographer has all the time he could want to look, think and record his holiday. The key to turning holiday snaps into good pictures is discipline—in the way you look at, and place your subjects in, your surroundings; in composition, viewpoint and lighting.

Introducing people

Pretty though some narrow village street may be, you will find that your pictures come to life if you include people. Don't be shy about it. Ask the local fishermen or the women talking in a doorway if you can photograph them. They can only say no and may be flattered.

In addition to local colour, you will probably want to take pictures of the people you are on holiday with. As most of us become self-conscious in front of a camera, try to catch them unawares. If that does not work, at least give them something to do, like sipping a drink or biting into a chunk of melon. Children will be at their best building sandcastles or splashing about in the water. Make your pictures tell a story and aim for a complete collection of place and family. Don't forget to include yourself: get someone else to take the occasional shot with you in it.

Viewpoint and lighting

Before you take a photograph, ask yourself two questions. Am I working from the best viewpoint? Is it the best light? Bright sunlight casts heavy shadows, which can be dramatic on buildings, but not on people. Try to avoid harsh midday sun in Mediterranean countries, the result will be pictures with too much contrast and unflattering shadows. Early morning or evening light brings out more delicate colours and long, gentle shadows. Don't be put off by bad weather. Medium-speed film can cope with most bad lighting conditions and the even, diffused light can be most flattering for portraiture.

Composing your picture

Having decided on viewpoint and lighting, give some thought to composing your picture. As your picture frame is not all that big you must make sure that every part is contributing to the whole. Skies can take up more space than anything else, so unless you are making a feature of them—a dramatic sunset, perhaps, or using them to emphasize a feeling of space—keep the amount of sky down to a minimum.

Sometimes your angle of view will leave you with an area of sky you cannot get rid of, resulting in a small image of a person overwhelmed by a large expanse of sky. Try to find some foreground to fill the space such as the bough of a tree. It may be out of focus, but that doesn't matter. Look out, too, for other frames—an arch or a gap between rocks are all useful. Not only do they give a picture shape, they also add depth.

▶ Right: look for ways to photograph people so they aren't staring into the sun. Here, water reflects light on to the face and required an off-the-face meter reading. *Michael Boys*

▶ Far right: here the bright light breaking through storm clouds throws up the shapes of the people clearly. *Adam Woolfitt*

▼ Below left: look for ways to combine colour and silhouette.

▼ Below right: this is a simple and very effective picture of a market stall-holder. The piles of fruit make a strong foreground.

Equipment

Travel light. It will be less restricting in the end. Keep equipment in a tatty holdall rather than a shiny new gadget bag.

Filters. Many photographers keep a skylight filter on the lens all the time. If you are shooting colour, it will reduce haze and the filter will protect your lens. It also helps to keep a lens hood on the camera. There is always the risk that the lens will pick up flare and spoil your picture.

Metering. Harsh lighting can be a very difficult problem in hot countries. If the picture includes both highlights and dense shade choose which is the most important and get as close as possible to take an exposure reading. A hand-held meter is more accurate than a through-the-lens meter in these extreme conditions.

Film. If you go to a sunny climate, you can afford to take slow-speed film— 100 ASA for colour slides, up to 200 ASA for colour prints and 125 ASA for black and white. If sunny weather isn't likely or you simply want greater latitude, Ektachrome 200 is a good medium-speed film for colour slides, Kodacolour 400 for prints (it's also balanced for both daylight and artificial light) and any 400 ASA film for black and white.

If you are taking candid shots of people it is unlikely that they will stay still for long and you will need to work quickly. Choose a film of at least 100 ASA to allow a shutter speed of 1/125 or faster. This will avoid camera shake and subject blur.

Lenses. If you are photographing in crowds it is easy to blend into the crowd and remain unnoticed. Details of expression or hand movements can be picked out with a long lens. A 200mm lens is about the longest that can be used in these cramped and crowded conditions. With a 35mm–105mm or 140mm zoom you will be equipped for a wide variety of shots.

Flash. It helps to have a small flash when working indoors or when there is mixed lighting. Use it as a fill in.

Precautions

Before beginning a holiday photographic session, there are a few things to remember. Keep the camera and lens clean and take plenty of film. Keep an extra

▲ Look for spontaneous moments that capture the spirit of a holiday. Keep your camera set at a fast shutter speed, such as 1/250, so you can be ready for when you need to stop movement. *John Garrett*

◄ Look for unusual viewpoints such as the top of a sea wall or a bridge. Here, the high camera position excludes unwanted detail while the wide-angle lens gives a feeling of immense space. *Roger Jones*

► Look for ways to emphasize the feeling of sun and brilliant light. A simple starburst filter here highlights the glitter of the sun and water. *Michael Busselle*

roll of film with you, either in a pouch on your camera strap or in your pocket (not in the glove box of the car). If you are at the beach, protect your camera from sand with a plastic bag sealed at the top with an elastic band and keep well away from sand and salt water which will jam up the mechanisms. If you do drop your camera in sand or salt water, take it to the nearest photographic shop straight away to be looked at. Rain water will not damage your camera so long as you wipe it dry as soon as you can.

Planning ahead

Taking your camera and equipment with you on holiday—particularly if you are going abroad—requires a certain amount of planning. Use the check-list below to remind you of all the things you should do before leaving home.

● **Insurance:** make sure your cameras and equipment are covered by holiday insurance.

● **Customs:** take receipts for your equipment with you in case you need to prove to customs on the way back that you did not buy anything abroad. Keep the receipts separately so that if your equipment is lost or stolen you will have a record of the camera body numbers and lens numbers. If you no longer have your receipts, take a copy of the insurance valuation and check with customs before you leave that this will be sufficient proof that you owned all photographic equipment prior to going away.

● **Security scanners:** some X-ray equipment used for security reasons at airports can damage film. Keep all your film together in your hand luggage and submit it for a visual check.

● **Film:** decide before you go what sort of film to take—and take plenty of it. Film can be expensive abroad, particularly in holiday resorts.

● **Insulated film bags:** heat breaks down film emulsion, so it is important to keep film cool. Take a cooler bag—Kodak makes one especially for the purpose—or take care to keep film in a cool place, such as a refrigerator, both before and after using it.

● **Lens cleaners:** take a blower brush or lens cleaning cloth to make sure your lenses are always clean. Take lens tissues and lens cleaning fluid to clean off fresh-water stains.

● **Notebook:** if you need a reminder of what you have taken photographs of, take a notebook and jot down captions as you go. You can also number each roll of film with self-adhesive freezer labels to help you to keep track.

▲ Look for new angles of traditional sights. Here, the photographer catches the reflections of a red double-decker bus in the breastplate of this guardsman.

◄ Look for ways to catch the magic of a place; *John Bulmer* waited until the water was perfectly still to take this mirrored reflection of man, camels and buildings. A 105mm lens keeps the proportions right.

▲ Look for local colour to bring back holiday memories. Here, the combination of the diffused lighting and the slow speed of Kodachrome produces fine detail and rich colouring.
Michael St. Maur Sheil

◄ Look for strong shapes and colours, effects that a simple 110 camera can capture as well as an SLR. A hard blue sky provides a vivid background for the brilliant reds and yellows of the Indian women's clothes. *S. G. Hill*

Photographing your garden

Every garden is full of subjects for your camera. Wide expanses of flower borders, separate plants and close-ups of individual flowers are only a part of the pictorial possibilities. The wild plants, which we call weeds, can be attractive also.

Pets are happy in the garden and so photograph well. There is always wild-life,—birds in abundance and variety, some welcome to the gardener like the robin, others enemies such as the pigeon, but all subjects for photographs. A bird table can attract the brightly-coloured tits and finches; also it keeps the birds in a small area so you can have the camera ready set up and focused. Damp places harbour fascinating frogs and even newts; these are always worth a picture. Insects are another facet of the pictorial wealth which can be found.

However, before you start snapping left, right and centre, take a few moments to have a good look around. Consider the overall view, the garden's shape and size, the way the house and garden relate. Some houses, hidden by creepers or trees, take second place to their gardens. With others, the solid mass of the house is balanced by the softer forms of nature.

The garden itself is full of contrasts: shape, volume, texture, light and shade, old and new. Consider your composition carefully. A focal point helps, both in close-ups and longer views. Apart from flowers and trees, there may be mossy paving you can use, an old wall, a fence or gate. Sheds and greenhouses make good subjects, and what's inside is often just as interesting.

Try taking photographs in all types of garden, from cosy cottage gardens bursting with old-fashioned herbacious plants and gnarled apple trees to large formal gardens such as you find at stately homes. A high viewpoint can portray their distinctive geometrical layout.

When to photograph

You can choose any time of the day or year to emphasize something special about your garden.

Morning The ideal time for general garden views is just after dawn when everything is fresh and dewy. Morning light is soft. There are no hard shadows and the air is usually still. This is a good time for flower studies.

Afternoon Unless the day is overcast (when light is low and there is little contrast) you will find that the higher sun causes shadows to become short and harsh. Colours record well in this bright light. If the light is diffused, objects can look two-dimensional without sufficient shadow to give them form. The best results are obtained on 'cloudy/ bright' days when there is some sun and blue sky, but enough cloud to soften and diffuse the light.

Evening Shadows are long, colours warmer. Lights come on—and this opens up new possibilities. Photographing at dusk, you may get the shapes of trees and house outlined against the sky, as well as glowing windows and lights.

The seasons also allow you to make the most of your garden.

Spring Flowering trees and shrubs can be photographed as a whole or in close-up—say, against a blue sky. Birds and insects are always around, so keep your camera handy. High-key pictures sometimes express the ethereal quality of spring light perfectly. Choose pastel colours, such as almond blossom, and over-expose by about a stop.

Summer This is the time to record beds and borders. But be careful of dark shadows. Get in close and concentrate on small groups of related colours. Pure light and shadow can be used for dramatic, contrasty pictures.

Autumn During this season shrubs and

▲ A 'cloudy/bright' day is best for garden shots when colours record full tonal range and lots of detail. Direct sun would make this shot too contrasty, putting the lower level in deep shade. A garden need not be carefully tended— this one, with its riot of overgrowth, echoes the slightly dilapidated-looking house behind. George Wright

▶ Spots of sunlight filter through to highlight the soft spring colours. The white cat makes a serene focal point, its colour balancing the spray of blossom above it. Derek Bayes used a 35mm lens and an exposure of 1/125 at f6·3 on 100 ASA film.

▶ Left: H. Gritscher used a 105mm macro lens to focus on the heart of this flower. An off-centre composition makes the shot more dramatic. Bright, but diffused, lighting accentuates the dazzling colour.
Centre: George Wright lets us into the secret of his garden shed! Studio flash with a diffuser attachment creates warm, hazy light to complement the window-lit composition. It also highlights the warm, autumnal colours.

fences are hung with spider-webs. In early morning water droplets shine on every leaf. Autumn leaves are a favourite subject, but pictures of whole trees can be disappointing no matter how colourful. Individual leaf shots are often more successful. Some of the most atmospheric garden pictures are taken when colours are softened by haze.

Winter Skies are usualiy grey and cloudy. Light is weak and diffuse. Although there isn't much colour, the delicate forms of twigs or dead leaves outlined in frost are simple and beautiful subjects. Everything glitters when the sun comes out, and gardens are transformed when it snows.

Necessary equipment

For most garden photos, you can use your basic SLR system, but for that *particular* one, you may need a little extra.

A moderate telephoto lens is good for birds and small animals. A standard or macro (50mm or 55mm) lens is fine for general shots. A macro lens focuses from infinity down to a reproduction ratio of 1:2 (half life-size). With extension rings it will give a 1:1 (life-size) ratio. A TTL meter compensates for the necessary exposure increase. To take in all of a small plot, a wide-angle lens (28mm or 35mm) is best. This is also good for dramatic effects like shooting up the trunk of a tree.

Flash 'freezes' flowers or leaves on windy days and isolates them from the background, which comes out dark. You can use fill-in flash to lighten shadows in small areas. Reduce the amount of flash normally required by one or two stops.

Because of the constant movement of most outdoor objects, a medium or fast film (100-400 ASA) is preferable. This allows faster shutter speeds.

▼ **Freshly-picked vegetables glistening with dew suggest an early morning shot. George Wright focused on the front tomatoes, giving limited depth of field and a blurred, contrast background.**

Exposure hints

For saturated colours, under-expose by at least half a stop if using slide film (say, for an indicated exposure of f11, set the aperture between f11 and f16). With backlit subjects, exposure according to the TTL meter reading gives a silhouette effect. For shadow detail, open up by one stop for slides or two stops for colour negative film (set f11 or f8 on an f16 reading). Bracketing the exposures—at half-stop intervals for colour, one-stop intervals for black and white—gives a choice of effects.

Outdoors with plenty of light and a fast film, it's tempting to work at small apertures. This gives maximum depth of field, but it can result in pictures with *too* much background detail. Press the preview button, if your camera has one, to check the effect at the taking aperture. Selective focusing simplifies compositions. Working at larger apertures (f5·6 or f3·5) can give romantic views framed by smudges of soft colour —out-of-focus leaves or flowers in the foreground. A telephoto lens gives the best results for small areas.

Using filters

A polarizing filter controls reflections from the surface of water. It also darkens blue sky and increases colour saturation by reducing glare. Keep the sun beind the camera for maximum effect. Remember, however, with a polarizer you'll need an exposure increase of one to two stops (The TTL meter takes this into account.)

A day-by-day record

To be really creative, photograph your garden every month, or every week, or even every day. This provides an interesting record of the changes in nature, as well as changes in your own life, and the use of your garden. Take your pictures from the same spot.

You will be amazed at the increase in your awareness—even if you only photograph your garden during the summer when you can be reasonably sure of good weather. But be aware, also, of the creative possibilities of the other times of the year. Not only glorious butterflies and intriguing caterpillars but also spiders in their dewy webs and a whole jungle of minature life wait to be discovered and recorded.

If you have no garden of your own, borrow those of friends and relatives. They may be amazed at how much you can find to photograph in them.

◀ A single electronic flash-gun and reflector captured this delicate lacewing fly hovering over a flower. The background is left in deep shadow, contrasting with the soft foreground colours. Mike Anderson used a 90mm/f2·8 macro lens on his Cosina CSR.

▶ A 'study in green'. George Wright's photo of cucumbers poking out under the edge of the whitewashed garden frame has little colour variety. But a strong composition using sharp contrasts of shape and line carries the picture. Wright used a 100mm lens at f16 to provide sufficient depth of field.

▼ Hidden in the shadow of a wall, this brightly-hued bed retains its pure colours, even when photographed on a dull day. George Wright set his camera on a tripod, exposing for 1 second at f22 on Kodachrome 25 film.

Photographing pets

Photographing pets is, in many ways, like photographing babies and young children. They will not always smile or look happy when you want them to. Nor will they sit or stand still on demand. This means you need a great deal of patience and quite a lot of knowledge about how the animal behaves—where his favourite haunts are, what sort of coaxing works, whether the animal will respond with an alert look to certain noises.

Be prepared to spend plenty of time on a session—perhaps an hour or two—and if the animal tires or loses interest, stop for a while and carry on later. There is no point in trying to force an animal to do something it doesn't want to do. The result will be an unhappy animal and unhappy pictures.

Equipment

This will obviously depend partly on what you have. But there are two lenses to avoid in certain circumstances. Don't use a wide angle lens for a head-on shot of animals with long noses, or you will get ugly distortion.

Don't use a standard lens for tiny animals or close-ups of a face unless your lens will focus closer than 1 metre. Otherwise, the animal will be too small in the finished picture.

An 85mm or 105mm lens can be useful if the animal is not moving around too much because it allows you to keep your distance and helps to cut out distracting background. Remember, though, that the longer your lens the shorter the depth of field. If you want depth of field, close the aperture up to f16 on a bright day and use a fast film.

Lighting and backgrounds

The garden is ideal for photographing cats and dogs. They will already feel at home there and it allows them space to roam around between shots.

Most animals have large shadow areas caused by noses, ears, tails and so on, so choose a shaded area or a bright overcast day. If you're shooting into a shaded area, expose for the shade. Keep the background uncluttered. For example, flower beds probably look too fussy but grass and blue sky make good backgrounds. Always focus on the animal's eyes and take your picture from a low viewpoint to avoid dwarfing the animal.

▶ Small animals look best against plain, contrasting backgrounds. Back lighting and a small aperture shows off the whiskers. *Sally Anne Thompson*

◀ A large aperture throws the background out of focus, but it also makes accurate focusing more critical. Always focus on the eyes. *Hans Reinhard*

▶ Cats seldom pose for the camera. You have to photograph them where you find them: be prepared for sudden movements.

▼ For action shots use a fast shutter speed (this spaniel was taken at 1/500) and focus quickly. If you can anticipate the animal's movements, set the focus beforehand and wait for the subject to come into view. *Sally Anne Thompson*

PHOTOGRAPHING PETS

Indoors, try to position the animal close to a window or open door with plenty of daylight coming through. Animals move quickly so unless you want to express this movement, use a fast film and a fast shutter speed—at least 1/250. It will help you to keep the animal in one place if you have someone holding it. At least one helper is always useful; this allows you to concentrate on your equipment while the helper looks after the animal. A trick often used by the professional animal photographers is to pre-focus on something—a leaf or a coloured ball, for example. When ready, tell the helper to release the animal and shoot your picture when it comes into focus.

● **Cats** should be photographed where you find them. In other words, take the camera to them and not the other way round. Cats are particularly receptive just after eating, when they are feeling contented and relaxed. Cats are also natural climbers so photographing them in a tree gives the picture a good background. But the cat may be hidden by leaves and branches so wait until it is climbing up a trunk which is relatively free of foliage. Put a bit of food in a branch and choose your lens, viewpoint and exposure settings in advance. Gentle noises will persuade a cat to look towards you—but make sure they are gentle. Too much noise will make it nervous. A squeaky toy or a quiet voice should be enough. If you use flash cubes and bulbs it can make animals nervous. Electronic flash is usually safe. If possible use the flash off the camera. Cats like the

▲ It takes a quiet photographer and a long lens to catch a cat napping. Here the photographer used a Pentax with a 105mm lens on Kodachrome.

▶ Most animals resent being dressed up: your reactions have to be very quick to catch moments like this.
▼ You often need help to control your subjects, but make sure the helper doesn't overdo it. Animals are quickly bored and walk away if they see the same routine too often. Contain playful animals in something: a white bucket also reflects light on a dark coat. *Anne Cumbers*

warmth of photo-floods so, if you can keep them in one place long enough, try some indoor shots with fixed lighting. And remember if you want to show your cat to best advantage, it will have its fullest coat of fur in winter. To photograph a black cat, you may need to increase the exposure by $1\frac{1}{2}$ stops. With a through-the-lens meter, take the reading directly on to the dark coat and fill the whole frame with the animal unless you are prepared to accept an over-exposed background. If you want some background, take a reading of both and expose mid-way.

● **Dogs,** particularly if they are well-trained, are the easiest animals to control. But this does not make them the easiest to photograph. Dogs are quickly excited and inclined to see the whole photographic session as a romp for their entertainment. This is, of course, particularly true of puppies. Try putting them into a container of some sort to confine them, or put them behind a log and be ready to press the button as they climb over the top. Dogs respond to a variety of noises and talking to them will often keep them still and attract their eyes to where you want them. A clicking noise from a window upstairs will generally win an alert expression. Don't try to tempt a dog with food or you will over-excite it.

▶ Here diffused light softens the background which, harshly lit, would be distracting. *Sheelah Latham*
▼ Fill-in flash helps to lighten dark fur, but it also pin-points eyes —especially of Siamese cats.

Sports and action photography

Fast films, zoom lenses, and the motion-stopping shutter speeds or flash of modern cameras make dramatic action pictures possible without special equipment. Most effective sports pictures are taken with ordinary SLRs and lenses between 24 and 200mm. It is often better to get close to an action subject, rather than stand back with a telephoto lens, because when you are close there is less chance of obstruction by spectators.

Flash, which is the best means for stopping action with simple cameras like 110, disc and 35mm compacts, can only be used up to about 5 metres. you can use it outdoors for subjects like bicycle stunts, and indoors for skating, martial arts and other events which allow you to stand fairly close.

Motor sport, air shows, team sports matches, track sports and river sports do require you to stand well back. The distance is usually related to the size and speed of the subject, so a standard zoom lens of 70-210mm is often perfect for all these events. You may find a longer lens useful for cricket, parachute displays, skiing and other sports where a fairly small subject has to be photographed from a considerable distance.

Frozen motion

To freeze movement, you must pick a shutter speed which limits the degree of blur produced so that it is not noticeable. If you can use 1/1000 or 1/2000, then almost any normal sports action will apparently be frozen perfectly. You would only notice the unsharpness if you enlarged the picture to poster size. For small prints, speeds like 1/250 or 1/500 will also 'freeze' fast action, but you will see that a runner's feet or the spokes of a wheel, which move faster than the rest of the subject, are blurred. Often this gives a good impression of speed.

Shutter speeds like 1/125 or 1/60 will not freeze action. Even a walking man will appear slightly blurred at 1/60 when crossing the field of view. Walking towards the camera, however, he would appear sharp. If you are forced to use slower shutter speeds, then try to shoot action subjects head-on. A good example is a group of cars coming round a banked bend on a track—the impression of speed will be there but because the motion is towards the camera, and not across the field of view, even 1/125 will freeze the subject sharply.

In many sports, the action has fast and slow phases and occasional 'stop points'. Pole vaulting is the textbook example. The vaulter runs, and rises up from the ground rapidly. Just as he goes over the pole there is a moment when he is almost perfectly still and balanced, before descending. If you can shoot at precisely this moment, then a shutter speed like 1/125 or 1/60 may show frozen action. The same applies to a somersault dive off a board, or to anything which goes up and then comes down. Another 'stop' is the moment of impact—when a boxer lands a punch.

Fluid motion

Sometimes sharply frozen detail does not convey the speed or movement in

▶ With his shutter set at 1/15, *Erich Baumann* went for an impressionistic shot of the dizzyingly fast sit-spin.

◀ *Tony Duffy* photographed Reiko Kubayashi performing a stag jump with flash-on-camera during a warm-up.

the subject even if it impresses by revealing details the eye misses. Using a longer shutter opening time, which may in turn mean a slower film on sunny days, you can follow the direction of action by 'panning' the camera. Panning means following the subject smoothly, camera pressed to your eye, swinging from the hip, and following through even after you fire. If you stop at the critical moment to press the shutter, you might as well have had the camera stationary all the time.

Try to forget you are firing the shutter, even if the viewfinder blanks out for a moment when you do. The best sports photographers keep their other eye open when looking through an SLR, as it helps make the pan action smooth. A panned shot can be taken at 1/30, 1/8 or even 1 second. As long as the camera tracks the subject perfectly, the subject will stay sharp; the background is turned to a speed-streaked blur. Any slight upward and downwards movement of the camera, or hesitation in the pan action, may also introduce shake or blur in the subject. Sometimes it looks better to have a slightly blurred subject as long as there is a core of sharp detail. A tripod with a swivelling 'pan' head or a monopod with a ball and socket head are invaluable supports for smooth panning, particularly with long lenses. Fluid movement can also be recorded by keeping the camera perfectly still and letting the subject record as a blurred track. This is less acceptable to most viewers. With indoor sports, you can sometimes fire your electronic flash with a 1 second long exposure, so that the film records two images—a sharp one, overlaid by a fluid blur. This is a very exciting way to capture the feel of action.

Framing and timing

Most viewfinders have a central focusing aid and it is easy to keep your subject lined up with this. Try to watch the edges of the viewfinder as well. It always looks better to have the subject coming into the picture rather than just leaving it, so pan your camera slightly ahead of the action, never lag behind. It takes at least 1/30 of a second between your pressing the shutter and the camera actually firing, so you should practice timing to catch peaks of action—you need to 'fire' well before the actual moment. Your own reactions are unlikely to be any quicker than the camera and this mental delay time has to be added on as well.

Winders and motor drives

The main benefit that an auto-winder has for action shots is that you do not need to take your camera away from the eye to wind the film on, as you do with a manual thumb lever. As auto winders only shoot between 1.5 and 2 frames

▲ Take a Fosbury Flop from behind the bar. Every 'flopper' jumps in a different way. Watch them in practice. Note how the bar is approached and which way they turn their heads. Straddle jumpers should be photographed from the front. Focus on the bar and wait for the jump. *Tony Duffy*

▶ Lucky shots cannot be planned for, but good timing can help. At the 1978 League Cup final, *Leo Mason* had just focused on the ball with Denis Tuart kicked the winning goal and he released the shutter by reflex. With a motor-drive this shot may have been lost.

each second, they are not fast enough to catch an action and guarantee you one 'peak' shot. The best timing might be exactly between the half-second intervals of the auto-winder's shots.

So you should still try to time each shot individually with an auto-winder. There are some slow-moving subjects, like a glider landing, where the 2 frames per second interval is adequate for shooting a sequence.

Motor drives run at 3 frames per second up to 5 frames per second (only special cameras are faster than this) and for most sports events, this is fast enough to avoid missing the best shot even if the film is allowed to run continuously. You should still time the shutter release point accurately, as it only takes 7 seconds to use a whole film with a fast motor drive. Keep your other eye open so that you can see enough of the action to know what is happening.

Pre-focusing

Most people find it easy to use a zoom lens to follow the subject in sports events, but focusing is much harder. Even experienced professionals hardly ever try to alter the focusing and follow a moving target. Instead, they study a dummy run (the last runner or the last lap) and see where the final subject is likely to arrive next time round, and where it will look best. It helps if there is a clear landmark like a road marking, a post or a hurdle to focus on carefully. After setting the focus on this marker, no attempt is made to refocus when the subject comes into view. Instead, you view it out of focus. As it comes to the 'action' point you will see it come into focus but you must not wait for this to happen before pressing the shutter! If you do, you will be too late and the subject will be caught just past your marker point, out of focus again. You have to time the release just as the action approaches the pre-focused spot.

This is another reason why motor drives are not as useful as they might seem for track sports—it is very hard to focus, zoom, pan and keep framing the subject correctly all the time while your motor drive takes a sequence of pictures. It is better to start the motor drive firing just as the subject approaches the marker.

Films for action

There are special films for sports and action photography, which allow much faster shutter speeds than ordinary high speed films. The most popular ones are Kodak VR1000 (colour negative, 1000 ASA) and Fujichrome 1600 (colour slide, 1600 ASA). There is also a Fujicolor negative 1600 ASA, a 3M transparency film of 1000 ASA, and a Kodak Ektachrome 800/1600 ASA. In black and white, Ilford's XP-1 and Agfa's Vario-XL can be used at similar speed ratings. These films are only suitable for action photography or

working in very low light, because in sunshine you will find it necessary to use 1/1000 and f22 for correct exposure on 1600 ASA film with light subjects, like water sports or skiing. This is the limit of most cameras' controls—some may have 1/2000th and some lenses have f32, but by no means all.

In bright light, then, you do not really need these very fast films, as a normal fast 400 ASA material will give considerably better colours, grain and sharpness and still allow 1/1000, 1/2000 or even 1/4000 of a second at very acceptable lens apertures. The ultra high speed films are only ideal for overcast weather.

For panned fluid-action pictures even this film speed can hamper you, making it impossible to use shutter speeds like 1/30, let alone 1/8th. This is one reason why most serious sports photographers carry two or three camera bodies, with different lenses and different films, to get all the effects and shots they want. At first you will have to experiment with one technique, one film, and one lens at a time, to find which suit you best.

Silhouettes

Some people take their first silhouette photos completely by accident. It is a common result of using an automatic camera to photograph someone standing in front of a window or a bright sky. The camera exposes for the background, so the subject comes out as a black, featureless lump. How disappointing! Nonetheless it is possible to use the same technique to create impressive pictures, like the ones here, on ordinary colour slide film.

The first requirement for a strong silhouette is *contrasty lighting*. If the lighting on the subject is the same as the lighting on the background, both will need the same exposure. The result will be an ordinary photograph. But if the subject is dark against a bright background, it is possible to produce a silhouette.

The easiest way to find this sort of difference in brightness is to position your subject against a bright sky and shoot directly into the light. The side of the subject facing the camera will then be in shadow—just what you want!

With colour slide film in the camera, take an exposure reading from the bright sky alone. This will lead to the subject being greatly underexposed, so it will come out as a silhouette.

Of course, it is also possible to take the same approach with negative films. The danger is that, when the prints are made, the operator may try to 'save' your pic-

▲ Helmut Gritscher took this shot of his son blowing bubbles. He set the exposure by metering only the bright sky. The setting sun lights up the bubbles as they are formed.

▼ Ashvin Gatha photographed his wife Flora in silhouette against a bright sky by finding a very low viewpoint. Her sari, blowing in the wind, adds interest to the shape.

ture. That is, he may try to rescue any detail which has been recorded in the main subject by greatly over-exposing the print. The result will be a wash-out. (Of course, one solution is to make your own colour prints!)

The second requirement for a strong silhouette picture is a *graphic design*. That is, the subject is shown so as to make the most striking impact that its shape allows. For example, a figure is shown in profile rather than head-on.

Go for side-on views of horses, bicycles, windmills and other subjects that have clear and interesting shapes from that particular angle.

Some subjects—such as trees or lighthouses—can be effective from any angle. With other subjects—including people—you may need to introduce an action, such as running or jumping.

If you can't get your subject higher up, try shooting from lower down. By crouching you can often show the essential shape of your subject against the clear background of the sky. That's an easy way to shoot a simple silhouette.

▼ **Peter Upton photographed the Brill Windmill—with cyclist—through two Hoya colour filters: an orange and a red 'centre spot' (red with a clear hole). He used a 105mm Nikkor lens. With pictures like this it is best to try several different exposures to make sure of getting one good result.**

Night photography

Taking your camera out at night can be more exciting and challenging than photographing by daylight, even—perhaps especially—when you leave your flash gun at home. The night photographer uses the lights that man and nature have devised to illuminate the darkness, which are more diverse and colourful than daylight. And photography thrives on variety.

During the day our eyes see clearly and we expect the camera to reproduce what we see. At night most people's eyes not only see a bare minimum, but often see it in less brilliant colour, less detail and with less clarity. The camera, however, can see colours which we cannot see at night, and look into dark shadows which our eyes cannot penetrate. One bright light in the darkness can prevent the human eye from adjusting to darker areas. The camera has no such limitations, and this is the beauty of night pictures.

Light sources

With a minimum exposure, the camera will only reproduce light sources: street lights, for example, car headlights (still or moving), lighted windows, signs, the moon and stars, reflections on water and so on. Fires, fireworks, TV screens and decorative illuminations are also all light sources. These subjects give us pictures of the colour, shape and movement of the lights themselves rather than any scenes they illuminate. Light sources can be photographed with fairly short exposures and there is often a choice between freezing moving lights or letting them make streaks of light on the film, as happens with moving car tail-lights.

The human eye does not normally see just the light sources: as well as all the neon signs at Piccadilly Circus or Times Square, we expect also to see detail of the buildings and streets. You can set your camera's highly selective exposure to leave out all this.

Lighted subjects

When photographing lighted subjects at night, minimal changes in exposure have more effect than on light sources. With more exposure, detail in the darkest areas becomes visible, while often the detail in lighter areas remains good as well. Moonlit scenes often look as bright as day, with blue skies, good colours, shadows with soft edges, and full detail—though the object with such pictures is usually not to simulate daylight but to go halfway to producing a night effect with good detail.

▲ Backlighting makes the most of this fountain by day, but its own lights give a far better effect by night. Note how long night exposure turns drops of water into a stream. *Dan Budnik*

▼ With a hand-held meter, *Robert Glover* had already worked out an exposure for a candlelit face (1/30 at f2 on 200 ASA film) so that for this shot he was free to watch for the right moment.

Light and subject

For some pictures you will want to show both the light source and the subject which it illuminates. The closer your subject is to the light, the better the result. Normally you will have to accept that the light will be slightly too bright while the subject is rather too dark, but an exception is where you use a reflective surface—a window or a wet street—to reflect the light source. A face has a slightly shiny surface and reflects better if you photograph it with the light behind it and slightly to one side—even including the light in your picture—than with the light coming over your shoulder. Instead of a dim, full-face portrait you will have a brighter, rim-lit profile, leaving the rest of the face in semi-silhouette.

Exposures

Exposures for night photography vary considerably, and the exposure you choose will depend on the scene and the effect you want. This makes it difficult to give precise guidelines for exposures though you may find the table of rough exposures overleaf useful as an initial guide. The table takes account of one complicating factor, known as reciprocity law failure.

▶ On 50 ASA daylight film, this shot was exposed for 30 secs at f22. Longer would have shown more detail on the tower but may have spoiled the balance, making the whirling lights too bright.

Reciprocity law failure refers to the fact that, with very long exposures, halving the aperture no longer has the same effect on exposure as doubling the shutter opening time. For exposures faster than 1/10, there is no problem. For exposures between 1/10 and 1 second, you should allow half a stop extra, and for exposures between 1 and 100 seconds allow between one and two stops extra. Always bracket exposures to be certain, preferably by altering the aperture setting rather than the shutter speed.

To complicate matters further, if you are working with slide films the density contrast and colour will change with different exposures. Trial and error is your best guide: take readings from different parts of the picture, allow extra time, make plenty of different exposures and keep notes on each one so that you can learn by experience.

With slide film, to get black shadows you must expose for the highlights: with negative film—colour or black and white—you need make fewer exposures because you can vary the effect by printing darker or lighter later on. Expose to give detail everywhere and then print to make the shadow black or detailed as you wish.

Meters

Most modern hand-held meters are of the CdS or silicon type and can get a reading in a lit night scene, but few TTL meters will. Even with the better TTL meters—Canon F-1 or Olympus OM-2—you should ideally use a hand-held meter as well. A few good hand-held meters will actually give a reading in moonlight.

As a general rule, if you want to record clear detail, measure the brightest part of the scene and allow three f stops more exposure, or eight times the shutter opening time, This method is equally effective with a hand-held meter or with a TTL meter used close up to the subject. TTL meters which take an average reading or are weighted towards the centre of the frame—but not spot meters—are also accurate for working out the exposure for neon signs and other light sources: move close enough for the sign to occupy one-third to half the picture and use the resulting setting from wherever you shoot the picture. Even with the best possible exposures, you should expect colour to change slightly, but your results will generally be creatively acceptable. Our own eyes do not see colours correctly at night.

Subject	Type of lighting	Effect	Settings (400 ASA film)
Street scene	strong city centre lighting, sodium or mercury vapour	dark	1/125 f4
		bright	1/60 f2·8
	small town, modest lighting	dark	1/60 f2·8
		bright	1/30 f2·8
Shop window	small store	normal	1/30 f2·8
	spotlit items	normal	1/60 f4
	very bright	normal	1/125 f4
Street lights Christmas lights	mixed	lights only	1/125 f8
		lights only	1/125 f5·6
		street as well	1/60 f4
Bonfire	wood	just fire	1/125 f4
		fire and faces of onlookers	1/60 f2·8
Fireworks	mixed	light source	1/60 f4
	sparklers	to illuminate face of holder	1/30 f2·8 45cm away
Car lights (rear)		light source	1/30 f2
		streaks	10 secs f8 50 mph
Neon signs		light source	1/60 f4
Floodlit buildings	various	normal	1/30 f2·8
Moonlit landscape	full moon	normal	20 mins f5·6
	half moon	normal	2 hrs f5·6
	full moon	moonlight	4 mins f5·6
	half moon	moonlight	20 mins f5·6
The Moon	clear night	detail surface	1 sec. f4 200mm lens

Film

You will get the greatest latitude for night photography by using a fast film, preferably 400 to 1600 ISO speeds. Fast film tends to be rather grainy, but it is better to get results with grain than no results at all. If you need still shorter exposures, all types of fast film can in fact be pushed to higher speeds: 400 to 800 ASA or 1600 ASA and in rare cases to 3200 ASA. With black and white film you can do this yourself by increasing the development times. Note: all exposures on the same film will be affected. With colour film, the enthusiastic experimenter can sometimes get good results from push processing, but processing laboratories offer special services which may be more reliable, though they cost two or three times the normal processing cost. Of course if you are using a tripod and can accept a blurred subject, you can use a slower film. For most night photography the make and type of film is not important. With colour slides, however, you may prefer to avoid the warm, rather orange tones that daylight film gives with floodlit shots, shop windows and other artificial lighting. To compensate for this use a blue (D to A) filter and give an extra stop on exposure, or load your camera with a tungsten balanced film—Agfachrome 50L, for example, or Ektachrome 160 Tungsten.

Equipment

A tripod is almost essential when photographing at night: choose one that is easy to set up with gloves on (some are very awkward indeed). Avoid small locking screws or adjustments. Never fix your camera to the tripod in the dark: fix it first in your car or indoors to avoid the risk of failing to thread it correctly without realizing it. Keep your camera in your car or under your coat as much as possible. If it gets too cold the shutter may become sluggish, and very cold weather can make the film brittle. Avoid loading film in the dark, or changing lenses (unless they are of a good bayonet type, with

locating warts). Never take your camera indoors from cold conditions with the lens removed: contrary to popular opinion, cameras do not mist up out-of-doors, but when they re-enter a warm, moist atmosphere. If misting does occur, leave any filter in place and never remove the lens or try to clean the mirror. Misting does no harm if allowed to evaporate normally. There are some useful aids to night photography: though only available light photography is discussed here, you may find a flash gun with illuminating dials useful for emergency viewing. A small torch is valuable, and so is the illuminating dial of an LCD watch: you can also buy inexpensive ballpoint

▲ *Eric Hayman* arrived at the exposure for this shot by taking a TTL meter-reading from the sky and then under-exposing it by 1½ stops to get the motorway in silhouette. With 64 ASA film this gave him 1 sec at f11.

◄ For a correct balance between the artificial light sources and the vestige of sky light, *Dan Budnik* had to bracket exposures—particularly as he was using Kodachrome which allows no leeway for adjustment in processing.

► *Robert Estall* took this shot of Piccadilly Circus on a 17mm lens open at f8 for 10 secs. This was long enough for a car to complete a right turn leaving a trail of yellow flashes.

▼ Mixed artificial lights can give un-predictable results: here *Laurie Lewis* used tungsten balanced film which has a bluish bias but copes well with lights ranging from floodlights to lasers.

pens which incorporate a torch for writing at night.

Few other accessories are needed. A watch—preferably with a second hand—is more important than any photographic extras. Some cameras have shutters with speeds up to 30 seconds, but most only go up to 1 second, and you will often need far longer exposures. One rather useful idea for night photography is the focusing light—a small torch fixed to your camera, aimed at the centre of the viewfinder's picture so that you can use the focusing screen at night. Another useful new idea is the auto-focus camera: some will not work at night, but others, particularly those with a light beam, can cope with darkness. The subject must be fairly central.

Darkroom work

Learning how to control the results from your camera is exciting, but it is even more absorbing to create the final images yourself, processing and printing your own films. You do not need to set aside a special room for this, as all you need today is an electricity supply and clean tap water.

The 'darkroom' can be replaced by a simple light-tight bag called a changing bag. You insert your arms into the sleeves of the bag after zipping your film and the developing tank into it. The film is removed from its cartridge, and wound into a plastic reel. Then the lid is fitted to the developing tank and you can remove it from the bag and work in normal lighting.

It takes about 20 minutes to process black and white or colour negative films, and about 40 minutes to process colour slides. You need to be able to give your full attention during this period, because the temperature of the solutions, keeping them moving over the film by agitating the tank, and the exact time you pour one out and the next in are all vitally important. You also need a clean, clear benchtop and the kitchen is often an ideal place to use if you keep everything well away from food.

As every process is different, the only way to learn the exact procedure is to study the instructions with the developing tank and with the chemical kit carefully. But all processes are similar; first, you treat the film in a developer which brings up the image; then you use a fixer which removes what remains of the original light-sensitive film emulsion; finally you wash the film to remove all the unwanted left over chemical residues; then you dry it.

This is the basic process for all negative films. For colour slides there are two additional baths between the developer and the fixer, sometimes three, and in all colour processes the fixer may be combined with or preceded by a bleach. But the principle is the same.

What matters is that you make the solutions up correctly with pure (or distilled) water, and store them properly in sealed airtight bottles. The tank and measures must be clean and you have to bring everything to the right temperature. Each solution must be used as directed, and there must be no cross-contamination. Finally, the water rinse at the end must be at the right temperature and the film must hang up to dry in a dust-free area, left undisturbed till fully dry.

If you think you can cope with these requirements, try black and white first (even just for a dummy run). Your dealer will fix you up with everything needed, often as a home darkroom package supplied complete by the maker. Colour slides have the advantage that once processed, you just need to cut them up and mount them to view them in a projector, so although slide processing takes longer than negative processing, it is the best process to tackle yourself to start colour.

Printing

To make your first prints, you either have to be able to black out a room, or invest in a daylight 'lab' printer. These are now very popular, though only recently introduced. They need no darkroom and stand on a worktop. The paper and chemicals for these printers is usually for printing from slides using a very simple one-bath process called Agfachrome Speed, with no critical temperature or time control.

Black and white printing is easy, as you can work in red safelighting and see everything happen in three open dishes, with no need for exact time and temperature. It is the best way to learn how photographic materials work.

You can buy a complete home black and white darkroom kit with paper and chemicals for the price of a budget SLR. Kits like this enable you to make enlargements up to 10 × 8″ from your own black and white negatives. Because black and white depends on judgment, your quality will only be as good as your expectations, and it does pay to visit a camera club and see what a good print should look like, or attend an evening class just to learn how to judge and control your results.

Colour printing from slides can be done using much the same equipment, or the daylight lab printer-processor, and the simplicity of the new rapid materials makes it very easy. You have the original slide to compare with your result, so you can tell if you are going wrong. Though more expensive than black and white, colour slide printing is often more successful for the first-time darkroom worker.

Printing from colour negatives is more complex. It calls for considerable skill in assessing tests and results, as colour negatives are impossible to 'read' by eye. You have to have a proper blacked-out darkroom, and apart from Kodak Ektaflex all the printing processes need very accurate control. the enlarger, electronic negative analyser and processing kit may cost more than your whole SLR outfit.

The cost of home colour printing is much higher than ordinary developing and printing costs, so it is only worthwhile for enlargements and exhibition prints. It can be very rewarding, but do not imagine that results are guaranteed; you need patience, concentration, manual skill and good subjective judgment. For colour printing from negatives you also really need a room you can use for two to three hours without interruption and this may limit your opportunities.

▶ A drying rack is easy to make. This one is a series of rectangular frames with a light muslin stretched over each. Ample space between the frames ensures good air circulation.

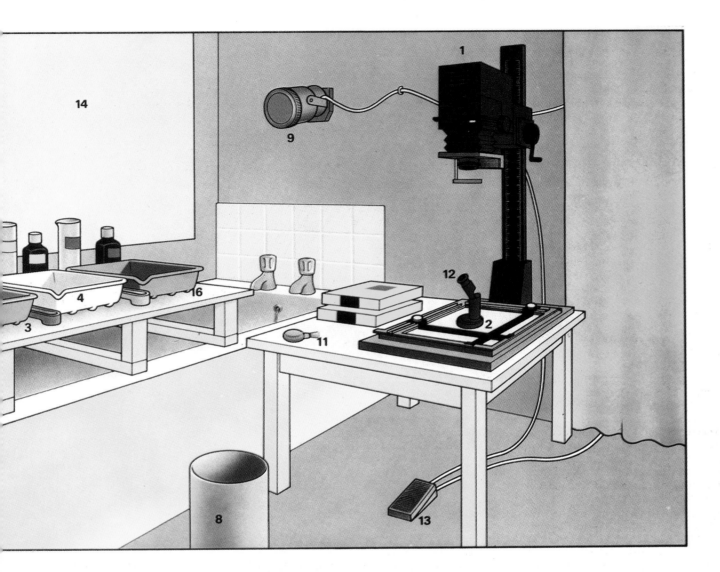

▲ A simple cabinet for making contact sheets. A safelight inside allows the paper and negatives to be positioned. A white light inside is turned on when the lid is down to make the exposure.

DARKROOM EQUIPMENT
Items marked with an asterisk are useful but not essential.

 1 enlarger
 2 enlarging easel* (masking frame)
 3 printing tongs
 4 developing trays
 5 graduates
 6 thermometer
 7 lint-free towel
 8 waste-bin
 9 safelight
10 timer with large dial
11 blower brush
12 focus finder
13 footswitch for enlarger* *or*
   exposure time switch*
14 blackout screen
15 ventilator hood
16 work bench
siphon for washing*, tray warmer*, enlarging meter*,
RC and flatbed print drier (glazer)*, print squeegee*

Displaying your results

There is little point in taking pictures if no-one sees them, and we are all so used to professionally presented images in the media that photographs do not easily catch attention.

A set of 35mm slides in a box or a wallet of colour prints is wasted, because you can not show them off properly in that form. The biggest mistake is to take out all the prints you shot, including the second best versions and the failures, and pass them round in a pack shuffled at random.

For prints, try using a small album with clear PVC leaves made to fit the shape of the print. Some companies will supply these with your prints at a small extra cost. Each album usually holds 24 prints, just about the right number if you have taken a 36 exposure film; most people would expect about 2 in every 3 shots to be worth keeping. The album makes it easy for people to see the prints, and keeps them in the order which you want them to be seen in.

Slides can be put in a plastic frame which holds 12, or a ring binder sheet which holds 20, and viewed with a simple magnifier. This is not ideal, but does let others see your work.

You can order prints from your slides, and some laboratories offer a service to process the film and make a print off every single slide at a reasonable overall cost. Then it is easy to keep the valuable original safely but have a set of prints to hand round in an album.

Pictures often gain impact when seen beside each other, and this is a strong argument for a larger album, normally with rigid leaves covered a tacky clear film which lifts off and drops back to secure any prints placed under it. You can arrange four prints on each page or have larger prints singly, and let your pictures tell a story with clarity.

In the home, put your favourite small prints in simple frames. Some neat ideas are available including picture packs which hold one print in the front, framed, with the rest of the set stored behind. Borderless glass frames cost very little, and so do picture cubes in perspex which hold six square prints. If you put a small print in a slightly larger frame, centering it on a mounting card, it will often look better. You can also trim it to improve the composition. It is much better, though, to order or make a selective enlargement which corrects the composition without cutting the print size down.

If you have never seen a large print from one of your shots, try it. There are some services which make prints 20 × 30″ or 30 × 40″ at very low prices, but these are often delivered loose, and can be hard to mount or display. It is better to order a block mounted 'heat-sealed' 20 × 16″ or 12 × 16″ print, which is firmly fixed to a fibreboard base and coated in a plastic laminate so that it will not fade, and resists moisture and damage.

Many photo dealers can also have your negative or slide made into a jigsaw, or into sets of place mats or coasters. Prints can be sealed into the base of a china plate, or removed from their normal paper base and bonded to artist's canvas before stretching over a wooden frame like an oil painting. These are just a few

1 Create thin black borders surrounded by white ones in the enlarger. The print is mounted on a lightweight block. 2 Metal frames complement vignetted images. 3 A sandwich of fibreboard, print and non-reflective glass held by clips. 4 Mount colour prints

of the interesting ways to put pictures into your home and make them more attractive.

Slide projection does not have to mean a darkened room and a big screen, though when done properly, the traditional method displays the remarkable sharpness and colour of slides off to the best advantage. You can use a small daylight projector with a built-in screen about 8″ square, so that several people can see the picture at the size of a larger-than-normal print.

You can also have your slides or prints put on to video cassettes by most dealers, to view them on your television as a continuous sequence. This is a good way to show wedding pictures, and it also means you can take slides to show a friend with a similar video player without having to bring a projector along. The quality is much lower than a projected slide.

Outside the domestic uses of your pictures, you may want to enter competitions or exhibitions. Once you decide to try this, you are not so free to vary the way the pictures are displayed. None of the interesting ways of treating your picture can be used; in magazine competitions, you normally must enter straightforward glossy prints no larger than 10 × 8″, or slides. Photographic societies often state that for a competition, every entry must be mounted on a 20 × 16″ card, and must not be framed. This is done in order to reduce everybody to the same level, to enable the real merits of the photography to be seen. Most people would consider the way pictures are mounted for photographic club contests unsuitable for any other display, whether in the home or in a local school or library.

There are ways to make such plain presentation effective. Any picture looks good if its glossy surface is perfect and unmarked, if the print is cleanly cut with a craft knife, and the mount is an attractive artist's mounting board in a dark neutral colour which helps the print stand out. A thin black border printed or cut using a secondary mounting sheet round the image can also look very professional.

Contest entries are received well if the packaging is sturdy, but easy to open, and the prints or slides can be removed and viewed without further unwrapping, and repackaged in your return envelope with little effort. Prints in envelopes sealed all round with two layers of tape, packed between two similarly taped cards, and wrapped in tissue paper are not popular. Slides

should be held in small vinyl pockets or sheets.

Finally, remember that only photographers are interested in the purely *photographic* quality of your pictures. Most people are far more interested in a good subject, to which photographic quality can be added as a bonus. Display your work to interest people rather than impress them, so that they enjoy the result rather than envy your skill or your equipment!

Negative files make it easier to locate and show your photographs.

Automatic focusing slide projectors focus electronically after the first slide has been done manually. These projectors also have a tape recorder socket and remote slide advance.

Index

Photographic acknowledgements

9 Richard Bradbury/Five Four Photography; Eaglemoss (top). 10 Eaglemoss (top); Jack Schofield (centre left); Fran Saunders (centre right). 11 Eaglemoss. 12 Eaglemoss (centre); Richard Bradbury/Five Four Photography. 13 Eaglemoss (top); Raymond Lea (bottom). 15 Richard Bradbury/Five Four Photography. 16 Richard Bradbury/Five Four Photography (top); Malkolm Warrington/Eaglemoss (lenses); Tina Rogers/Eaglemoss (chess pieces). 17 Richard Bradbury/Five Four Photography. 18 Malkolm Warrington/Eaglemoss (top). 19 Richard Bradbury/Five Four Photography (top); Fujimex (bottom). 20 Colour Library International (left); Malkolm Warrington/Eaglemoss (right). 21 Malkolm Warrington/Eaglemoss (top), Marc Riboud/John Hillelson (bottom). 22 Malkolm Warrington/Eaglemoss (top). Alfred Gregory (bottom). 23 Malkolm Warrington/Eaglemoss. 24, 25, (centre); Michael Basselle (bottom); 30, 31 Michael Taylor/Eaglemoss. 32, 33 Michael Busselle/Eaglemoss. 34, 35 Con Putbrace/Eaglemoss. 36 Barry Lewis/Eaglemoss. 37 Barry Lewis/Eaglemoss (left); Brian Brake (right). 38 All Sport (top), Barry Lewis/Eaglemoss (bottom). 39 Barry Lewis/Eaglemoss. 40 Richard Bradbury/Five Four Photography. 41 Ron Chapman. 42 Con Putbrace/Eaglemoss. 43 John Meek (top); Suzanne Hill (centre); Peter Myers (bottom). 44 Eaglemoss. 45 Ricardo Gomez Perez. 46 Ricardo Gomez Perez (top); Malkolm Warrington/Eaglemoss (bottom). 47 John Garrett (top); Malkolm Warrington/Eaglemoss (bottom). 48 Malkolm Warrington/Eaglemoss. 49 Ricardo Gomez Perez (top). 50 Ricardo Gomez Perez (top); Malkolm Warrington/Eaglemoss (bottom). 51 Malkolm Warrington/Eaglemoss; 52 Richard Bradbury/Five Four Photography. 53 David Kilpatrick/Eaglemoss. 54 Aspect (top); Roland Michaud/John Hillelson (centre); Don Morely/All Sport (bottom). 55 Julian Calder/Susan Griggs Agency (top); Bruce Coleman Ltd (bottom). 56–57 Gerry Cranham. 57 John Garrett (top); John McGovern (centre); David Kilpatrick. 59 John Evans. 60 David Kilpatrick. 61 Heather Angel. 62 J. Pfaff/ZEFA. 63 Sanders. 64, 65 John Evans. 66, 67, 68, 69 Steve Bicknell/Eaglemoss. 70 Malkolm Warrington/Eaglemoss. 71 Eric Crichton (top left); Malkolm Warrington/Eaglemoss (top right); Heather Angel (bottom). 72, 73 Eric Crichton. 74 Richard Bradbury/Five Four Photography. 75 Christopher Angeloglou (top, centre bottom and bottom right); Philippa Longley (centre top left and centre bottom left); Steve Bicknell/Eaglemoss (bottom left). 76 Alfred Gregory (top left); Eric Crichton (top right); Christopher Angeloglou (bottom). 77 Con Putbrace/Eaglemoss (top); Hans Reinhard/Bruce Coleman Ltd (bottom). 78 Michael Boys/Susan Griggs Agency. 79 David Kilpatrick (top); Hoya Filters (centre); Tony Jones/Robert Harding Library (bottom). 80 David Kilpatrick (top left and bottom); Hoya Filters (top right); 81 Hoya Filters. 82 Malkolm Warrington/Eaglemoss (left), Raul Constancio (right). 83 Malkolm Warrington/Eaglemoss. 84 Jill Richards (top); Hoya Filters (bottom). 85 Peter Goodliffe (top); Lisa le Guay (bottom). 86 Lisa le Guay (top); Hoya Filters (bottom). 87 Lisa le Guay (top); Malkolm Warrington/Eaglemoss (bottom). 88 Lisa le Guay (top); Malkolm Warrington/Eaglemoss (centre); Martin Riedl/Eaglemoss (bottom). 89 Martin Riedl/Eaglemoss (top); David Morey (bottom). 90 Hoya Filters (top); Derek Bayes/Aspect (bottom). 92, 93 Colour Library International. 94, 95 Michael Busselle. 96 English Scene (bottom); Alex Langley/Aspect (top). 96, 97 Ernst Hass/Magnum. 97 John Garrett (top); Suzanne Hill (bottom). 98, 99 ZEFA. 100, 101 Ken Kirkwood/Eaglemoss. 102, 103 Mike Newton. 104 Robert Estall (top), Eric Crichton (bottom). 105 Martin Parr. 106 John Bulmer (top); Eric Stoye (bottom). 107 Bryn Campbell/John Hillelson. 108 John Bulmer (top); Roland Michaud/John Hillelson. 109 Tomas Sennett/John Hillelson (top); Patrick Ward (bottom). 110 Malcolm Aird. 111 Andrew Evans (top); Patrick Thurston (bottom). 112 Lawrence Lawry (top); Anne Conway/Eaglemoss (bottom). 113 Ed Mullis/Aspect (top); John Garrett (bottom). 114 Steve Herr/Vision International. 115 Paolo Koch/Vision International (top); John Bulmer (bottom left); Lisa Mackson (bottom right). 117 Clive Sawyer/ZEFA (top); Mike Newton (bottom). 118 Adam Woolfitt/Susan Griggs Agency. 119 Michael Busselle. 120 Bruno Barbey/John Hillelson. 121 Michael Busselle. 122 Eric Crichton (top); Suzanne Hill (centre left); Michael Busselle (centre). 123 Michael Busselle (top left, centre left); Ardea (top right); Colin Barker (centre right); Cressida (bottom right). 124 Michael Busselle (top); Herbie Yamaguchi (bottom). 125 Michael Busselle (top and bottom right); Herbie Yamaguchi (bottom). 126 Michael Busselle (top); Robin Laurance (bottom). 128 Sanders. 129, 130, 131 Tino Tedaldi/Eaglemoss. 132, 133 Helmut Gritscher/Aspect Picture Library. 134, 135 John Garrett. 136 Spike Powell (left); James Carmichael/The Image Bank (right). 137, 138 Steve Bicknell/Eaglemoss. 139, 140 John Hillelson Collection (top), Howell Conant/John Hillelson. 141 Richard Greenhill (top); Clay Perry (bottom). 142 Richard Greenhill (top); The Picture Library (bottom). 143 Gered Mankowitz (top); John Bulmer (bottom). 144 Martin Riedl/Eaglemoss (top). 145, 146 Colour Library International. 147 Colour Library International (bottom): Michael Busselle (top). 148 Colour Library International. 149 Tino Tedaldi (top centre and right); James Wedge (top left). 150 Derek Bayes/Aspect Picture Library. 151 Derek Bayes/Aspect Picture Library (top); Michael Boys/Susan Griggs Agency (bottom); 152 John Sims (top); Archie Miles (bottom); 154 Georg Gerster/John Hillelson. 155 Peter Goodliffe. 156 Peter Goodliffe, Barry Lewi; 157 Bill Coleman. 158 Jean Bichet/The Image Bank. 159 Sergio Dorantes. 160 Colin Molyneux. 161 Marshall Smith/The Image Bank. 162 Marc and Evelyne Berheim/Woodfin Camp. 163 Adam Woolfitt/Susan Griggs Agency (top right); John Garrett. 164 Roger Jones/English Scene. 165 John Garrett (top); Michael Busselle (bottom). 166 John Bulmer. 167 Robert Harding (top left), Michael St Maur Sheil Susan Griggs Agency (top right); S. G. Hill (bottom). 168 George Wright. 169 Derek Bayes/Aspect Picture Library (top); George Wright (bottom). 170 Mike Anderson (top); George Wright (bottom). 171 George Wright. 172 Hans Reinhard/Bruce Coleman Ltd (top); Sally Anne Thompson (bottom). 173 Julian Calder/Susan Griggs Agency (top); Sally Anne Thompson (bottom). 174 Christopher Angeloglou (top); Sally Anne Thompson (centre, bottom left); Anne Cumbers (bottom right). 175 Sheelah Latham (right); Sally Anne Thompson (left). 176 Tony Duffy/All Sport. 177 Erich Baumann/All Sport. 178 Tony Duffy/All Sport. 179 Leo Mason. 180 Helmut Gritscher/Aspect Picture Library (top); Ashvin Gatha (bottom). 181 Peter Upton. 182 Dan Budnik/John Hillelson (top); Robert Glover (bottom). 183 Colour Library International. 184 Dan Budnik/John Hillelson. 185 Eric Hayman (top); Robert Estall (centre); Laurie Lewis (bottom). 187 Barry Lewis/Eaglemoss. 188 John Kelly (top centre); Kim Sayer (top right); Horner Sykers (top left). 189 Newnes Books